WOMEN'S HISTORY: TRIVIA, FIRSTS & OTHER MUSINGS

Volume I circa 1438 through 1799

PAULA C. HENDERSON

THE WOMENS HISTORY TRIVIA BOOK

ISBN: 9798437709870

Contents

FIRST, A FEW THINGS 3

1500 5

1600 6

1700 16

1701 17

   MUSING 17

1702 17

1705 18

1708 19

1713 19

1715 20

1717 20

1720 20

1721 21

1724 21

1725 22

1726 22

   MUSINGS 22

1728 23

1729 23

1731 24

1732 24

1733 25

1735 26

1736 28

1737 30

1739 31

1740 31

1741 31

1743 32

1744 33

1745 33

1748 34

1750 34

1752 35

1753 35

1754 36

1755 39

1756 39

1758 39

1759 40

1760 43

1761 43

1763 44

1766 44

1767 45

1768 46

1769 46

1770 49

1771 49

1772 50

1773 51

1774 54

1775 58

1776 60

1777 64

    MUSINGS 76

1778 76

1779 78

1780 79

    MUSINGS 79

1781 80

1782 81

1783 85

1784 86

1785 88

    MUSINGS 88

1786 88

1787 90

1788 90

1789 91

1790 99

1791 105

1792 108

1793 111

MUSINGS 121

1794 121

1795 124

1796 126

1797 126

MUSINGS 130

1798 130

MUSINGS 131

1799 132

The 1800s..137

ABOUT THE AUTHOR 137

The information herein

of women's history

is listed in chronological order

as it happened.

A special thank you to :

Wikipedia.com
Newspapers.com
chroniclingamerica.loc.gov
whitehouse.gov
britannica.com
womenshistory.org

And, a very special thank you to each and every woman in history.

FIRST, A FEW THINGS

Much of what you will read includes actual articles from newspapers (italicized gray quoted text). This not only gives us facts and trivia but allows us some insight into the actual attitude of society towards women in a given year. Women and men reading the newspaper at that time can see what is being said about women in their respective newspapers. This most definitely can influence opinions as well as spawn protests.

As we begin our journey through women in history much of the news in Volume I is out of England as the 'New World', aka United States, has not been formed. As we move through the decades this books focus will be more narrowed to women's firsts in the United States but certainly not limited to that narrative. Women's firsts from all over the world are included in this series with a main focus on the United States in later Volumes once America has been formed.

This Volume I includes 106 women who became newsworthy for one reason or another in our history and they are from all over the world and various walks of life.

1.   In **195 BC** in Ancient Rome one of the earliest documented protest occurred when a law was passed forbidding women from having more than half an ounce of gold and another law that dictated their dress and limiting their boundaries within the city. The women "stormed the house of commons" in protest of these restrictions.

SUFFRAGETTES IN OLD ROME

Prof. Frank J. Abbott says in his "Society and Politics in Ancient Rome" that suffragettes made their first appearance in politics in 195 B. C. The object of the uprising was the law that forbade a woman to have more than half an ounce of gold, to wear a parti-colored gown or to ride in a chariot within the city limits or within a mile of it, except for religious purposes. The ladies rose up in wrath and denounced such a law, storming the forum just as the new suffragettes have stormed the house of commons. They blocked all the streets of the city leading to the forum and asked each man as he approached to vote to restore their rights to them.

St. Tammany Farmer, Covington, Louisiana, December 25, 1909

2. *1438* – In the year 1438, **Margery Kempe**, an author, is touted as having written the **very first autobiography in English.** The exact date of her birth and death are not known but it is believed her book was written in 1438 just prior to her death. Excerpts of the book are rumored to have been published in the early 1500s, but the book was not published in its entirety until it was re-discovered in 1936. A statue of Margery Kempe was erected in 2020 at the entrance of a medieval bridge in Oroso, Northern Spain.

3. *1492* – (Spain) '**Queen Isabella the 1st'** gave approval, and financed the exploratory voyage made by Christopher Columbus in the year 1492. When he returned to her with Indians he had kidnapped for slaves, as a gift to the Queen, she ordered him to immediately return them and release them to their rightful freedom. During her 30 year reign, from 1474-1504 Queen Isabella reorganized her countries system of government. Spain's crime rate went down and the debt left incurred by King Henry IV was relieved. While she was against slavery, she did have her prejudices when it came to religion, and expelled the Jews from Spain that refused to convert to Christianity.

1500

4. *November 26, 1504* – **Queen Isabella I** dies. She is 53 years old. Her successor is another woman, her daughter, Joanna of Castile, also known as Joanna the Mad or in Spanish, Juana la Loca. She will reign until 1555.

5. *1517* - It is accepted opinion that Leonardo da Vinci finished the Mona Lisa painting in the year **1517**. History tells us the portrait of **Mona Lisa** is the result of Leonardo being commissioned by the patriarch of the Gherardini family that lived in Florence, Italy. **Lisa del Gherardini** married Francesco del Giocondo in 1495. Her husband paid Leonardo to paint the portrait of his wife, Lisa. Lisa died circa 1551 at age 70-72 The Italian name for the painting, originally, was called La Gioconda.

6. *1568* - **Maddalena Casulana**, an Italian song writer who lived in Florence, Italy between the years **1544 and 1590** published her first book of madrigals in 1568. Making her **THE FIRST WOMAN** to have her music published. A total of 66 of her madrigals survive.

Here is an article I found in The Winnipeg Tribune, Canada dated Sept 27, 1919 that mentions **Maddalena Casulana**: *"With the development of *contrapuntal music, women composers of higher position began to appear. In the 1500s they were to be found in many countries. Italy offered Maddalena Casulana, Vittoria Alcotti, Francesca Caccini (daughter of the operatic pioneer, Cornelia Calegari Catterina Assandra, and several others who composed motets, madrigals and finally operas. France boasted of Clementine de Bourges, a really gifted composer. The unfortunate Mary, Queen of Scots showed the influence of French models in some of her songs, which were successful in their day. Madelka Bariona was a German composer of the same period. Another* *remarkably gifted woman was Bernada de Lacerda, of Portugal, to whom Philip II wished to entrust the education of his children.*

From that time to the present the list of women composers is fairly continuous. The change from counterpoint to the harmonic style found the women ready to meet the new conditions, Francesca Caccini and others in Italy composing operas as well as madrigals. France, too, soon became a home of opera, and Elizabeth Claude de la Guerre won some success in this field, earning the respect of Louis XIV." ~ The Winnipeg Tribune, Canada

7. *1587* - **Virginia Dare** is reportedly the **first white English child born in the Americas** when she was born in Roanoke, Virginia in the year **1587**.

8. *1595* - Pocahontas, assumed to be born in the Tidewater region of Virginia was born circa 1595 within the Powhatan Indian Tribe.

1600

9. *1607* - By 1607 Jamestown, Virginia has been settled and in 1608 **Anne Burras** becomes the **first documented white English woman** to marry in the "New World". She arrived in the New World with a ship load of supplies in the employ as a maid to Mrs. Thomas Forrest. Within the year she married John Laydon and they had four daughters: Virginia, Alice, Katherine, and Margaret. Her daughter, Virginia Laydon is the first child born in the new English colony of Jamestown.

A statue of Anne Burras can be found at the Virginia Women's Monument erected in 2018-2019 located at the Virginia State Capitol. The tribute also includes life size statues of Cockacoeske, Mary Draper Ingles, Elizabeth Keckley, Mary Todd Lincoln, Laura Copenhaver, Virginia Randolph and Adele Goodman Clark.

---

10. *1613 -* **Pocahontas**, who had, by all accounts, been helping the Jamestown Colonist to secure much needed food and supplies and acting as liaison between the white colonist and the Indians was kidnapped by the colonist in 1613. They held her for ransom after what was considered a hostile event between Captain John Smith and her tribe. They baptized her, giving her the name Rebecca. Whether or not this was against her will is not known. What we do know is that in April of **1614** she married tobacco farmer John Rolfe. They had a son, Thomas in January of 1615.

11. In **1617, Pocahontas**, her husband, John Rolfe, and their young son travelled to England with anticipation of meeting the Queen. The Queen consort of England at this time was Queen Anne of Denmark, married to King James I.

12. **Pocahontas** passed away in March of 1617 while still in England. She was buried at Gravesend, England where her grave remains today albeit lost after the nearby parish burned down. She was between 20 and 21 years of age at the time of her death. A statue of Pocahontas stands outside the St. George Church in Gravesend, Kent, England. In 1907 she will become the first Native American to be honored on a U.S. postage stamp.

Pocahontas. Oldest portrait hanging in the National Portrait Gallery.
Painted of Pocahontas during her trip to London in 1616.

13. *1619* - Back in Jamestown, Virginia, the first slave ship arrives on the shores of the New World in 1619, this, and the ships that follow for the next 241 years would culminate into approximately six million slaves in the United States. We can approximate that about half were women.

14. *1634* - **Enter Anne Hutchinson**. Remember that the whole purpose of the "New World" was to have religious freedom and yet when Anne Hutchinson showed up she challenged what the colonist's true desire was for the New World. Anne hosted women at her home speaking the 'Free Grace' or Antinomians theology. The simplified version is that Anne Hutchinson preached a covenant of grace while the colony Puritans preached a covenant of works.

15. *In 1637* - Hutchinson was arrested for her "unorthodox" teachings. She was convicted and banished from the colony. She, her eleven children and many of her followers established Portsmouth, Rhode Island. As threats loomed of Boston attacking Portsmouth, Anne and half of her children moved to Split Rock, now known as The Bronx, New York. This turned out to be a fatal error. At this time hostilities abounded with the nearby Siwanoy Indians and in August of **1643** Anne, and all but one of her children in Split Rock were killed during the Kieft's War.

Susanna, her nine year old daughter was the lone survivor.   Anne is remembered in Massachusetts for her courage to exercise her civil liberties in the face of those less tolerant. Did the English Colonists really flee England believing in an individual's freedom of religion or did they come only to do exactly what England was doing to them; forcing one religion on everyone? Anne Hutchinson played an important role in our history being **the first woman (person) to challenge the truth about what "freedom of religion" really means.**

Anne's daughter Susanna returned to the Boston area to live with her remaining siblings that didn't go to Split Rock. She married when she was 18 and had a family. Her and her husband, John Cole had settled back in Rhode Island by 1663. Her husband passed away in 1707 and Susanna died on December 14, 1713 at age 80.

16. *In 1647* Maryland, a 46 year old recent immigrant from England named **Margaret Brent** became the **first female land owner in Maryland** when her brother transferred 1000 acres of land to her on Kent Island, Maryland. Add to that the land her brother inherited by his marriage to **Mary Kittamaquund** who had inherited tribal lands when her father passed away.

17. During this time Margaret Brent had become close friends with the then Governor of Maryland, Leonard Calvert. When he died in June of 1647, Margaret was named executor of his estate. Margaret has long since been considered the **FIRST SUFFRAGIST IN MARYLAND** since demanding her right to vote before the Maryland Legislation as the executor of Leonard Calvert's Estate. "I've come to seek a voice in this assembly. And yet because I am a woman, forsooth I must stand idly by and not even have a voice in the framing of your laws" **Her request was denied.**

First Suffragist

Voter, Needham—It is said that the first woman to demand suffrage was probably Mistress Margaret Brent of Maryland, in 1647. She was the heir of Lord Calvert, the brother of Lord Baltimore. As representation in the Legislature of Maryland was based on property, she demanded "place and voice" in that body. Her petition was hotly debated and finally refused.

The Boston Globe, Massachusetts

This occurred during the English Civil War which, by now, had moved into Maryland. Gov. Calvert died before paying the soldiers that had protected his estate as well as the colony. Margaret fed, clothed and paid the soldiers, took in rents due the estate and paid the debts.

Margaret Brent never married. She died in 1671.

18. *1648 –* "In 1648 **Margaret Jones** was indicted for being a witch, found guilty and executed. This was the **first instance of capital punishment for witchcraft** in New England." ~ The Pittsfield Sun, Massachusetts, Oct 3, 1822

19. *1650* - According to the Poetry Foundation **Anne Bradstreet was the first woman** to have her poems published in the Americas. Her most celebrated volumes, "The Tenth Muse Lately Sprung Up in America" was published in **1650**. Born in England around 1612, she died in 1672 in Massachusetts.

20. *1659 –* "In 1659 Marmaduke Stephenson, William Robinson and **Mary Dyer**, Quakers, were brought to trial before the general court of Massachusetts and sentenced to death. Robinson and Stephenson were executed. They received this sentence for their rebellion, sedition and presumptuous obtruding themselves after banishment under pain of death.

    Mary Dyer was reprieved on condition of her departure from the jurisdiction in 48 hours, and if she returned to suffer the sentence. She returned in 1660 and was executed." ~ The Pittsfield Sun, Mass, Oct 3, 1822

21. *1660s –* The early English stage only allowed men to act. They even portrayed the female roles. Finally, in the early **1660s** women were permitted to act on stage in England. **Mary Saunderson became the first woman** to play Shakespeare's Juliet on the English stage.

wikipedia.org/wiki/Mary_Saunderson,

npg.org.uk/whatson/the-first-actresses/first_actresses_exhibition/first-actresses-explore

22. *1660* - **Mary Dyer** was hanged in Boston for practicing the Quaker religion in colonial Puritan America. The Puritans had banned the Quaker religion. She was just one of four, now known as the Boston Martyrs. The Court documents the exchange between then Governor Endicott and Mary Dyer as follows:

"**Endicott**: Are you the same Mary Dyer that was here before?
Dyer: I am the same Mary Dyer that was here in the last General Court
Endicott: You will own yourself a Quaker, will you not?
Dyer: I own myself to be reproachfully so called.
Endicott: Sentence was passed upon you the last General Court; and now likewise. You must return to the prison, and there remain till tomorrow at 9 o'clock. Then you must go to the gallows and there be hanged till you are dead.
Dyer: This is no more than what thou sadist before.
Endicott: But now it is to be executed. Therefore prepare yourself tomorrow at nine o'clock.
Dyer: I came in obedience to the will of God the last General Court, desiring you to repeal your unrighteous laws of banishment on pain of death and that same is my work now, and earnest request, although I told you that if you refused to repeal them, the Lord would send others of his servants to witness against them."

It is assumed Mary Dyer was about 49 years old at the time she was hanged. So much for religious freedoms in the New World.

A statue of Mary Dyer was erected in 1959 outside the Massachusetts State House in Boston. The statue was sculpted by Sylvia Shaw Judson.

In 1661 the King sent a letter to the Governors in New England directing them to cease all executions and imprisonments of Quakers. Subsequently, the Puritans passed a new law called The Cart and Tail Law wherein they would tie suspected Quakers to carts, strip them to the waist and drag them through town behind the cart.

---

*The people that settled here so they would not be
persecuted for their religion are now persecuting
others for their religion.*

Quaker persecution finally stopped later in the 1670s when public
sentiment had begun to change.

23. Sculptor **Sylvia Shaw Judson** (B:1897-D:1978) sculpted a seven foot
statue of Mary Dyer in 1957, erected at the Massachusetts State
House in Boston. Sylvia Shaw Judson gained posthumous notoriety
when her statue, Bird Girl, sculpted in 1936, was featured on the
book cover and opening scene from the famed book and movie,
'Midnight in the Garden of Good and Evil, filmed on location in
Savannah Georgia. The statue, Bird Girl is located in Savannah's
Bonaventure Cemetery. An original bronze copy of Bird Girl recently
sold at action in 2021 for more than $390,000! Other works of Sylvia
Shaw Judson:

- Naughty Faun, Chicago Botanic Garden (1923)
- Merchild, Chicago Botanic Garden (1925)
    - Little Gardener at the Jacqueline Kennedy Garden at the White
      House (1929)
    - Girl with a Squirrel at the Brookgreen Gardens, South Carolina
      (1932)
    - Young Woman Dayton, Art Institute, Dayton Ohio (1934)
    - Bird Girl located at the Telfair Museum of Art in Savannah, GA
      and at the Ryerson Conservation Area in Riverwoods, Il (1936)
    - Girl with Piglet at the Brookfield Children's Zoo in Brookfield,
      Illinois (1960)

She has over 30 statues on display around the United States.

24. *1664 –* In 1664 **Margaret Fell** was arrested for failing to take an oath to the King and for allowing Quaker meetings to be held in her home. She was imprisoned for more than four years. While in prison, Margaret wrote the pamphlet, 'Women's Speaking Justified Proved and Allowed of by the Scriptures'.

25. *1667 -* **Abiah Folger, mother of Benjamin Franklin, is born in 1667 in Nantucket, Massachusetts.** Her mother, Mary Morrell Folger (grandmother of Benjamin Franklin) was born in England and came to the Americas by being an indentured servant. Indentured servants would agree to work for a period of usually seven years as a way to pay the cost of transportation to the colonies of the New World. Indentured servants could be sold but were otherwise free to move about, marry, etcetera but not runaway prior to working off said contract.

26. Abiah's sister Bethshua Folger was directly involved with the Salem Witch Trials, reportedly accusing some and throwing a shoe at an accused persons head during one of the trials. Bethshua claimed hysterical blindness during another trial as proof an accused was in fact a witch. Abiah Folger will go on to marry a candle maker, Josiah Franklin and they will have ten children, one of which is Benjamin Franklin. There is a monument to Abiah on Madaket Road at the location of what was the Folger Farm which is now owned by the Nantucket Historical Society Association.

27. *May 25, 1673 -* In **1673** a woman named **Ann Marwood Durant became the first woman** known to act as an attorney in a North Carolina court of law.

She and her husband settled on what is now known as Durants Neck which the Durants originally purchased from the local Indians.

Records show that Ann appeared in court on May 25, 1673 and successfully defended seaman Andrew Ball in a case filed to collect his unpaid wages.

ncpedia.org/biography/durant-ann

28. *1675* - **Maria Sibylla Merian** published **her first book** of insect illustrations in 1675.

   Born in 1647 Germany, she became a pioneering woman in the world of entomology. She was not only known for her beautifully detailed illustrations of insects and plants but for her work in identifying new species and the mysterious behaviors of certain insects. She documented in great detail the process of metamorphosis at a time when many still believed that bugs merely "came up out of the ground".

   wikipedia.org/wiki/Maria_Sibylla_Merian

   britannica.com/biography/Maria-Sibylla-Merian

29. *1677* - Back in the 'New World' it is **1677** and a female Pamunkey Indian Chief named **Cockacoeske**, known by many as the **Queen of the Pamunkey** had emerged before the House of Burgess in Jamestown asking for the release of Pamunkey people taken captive during an attack by Nathaniel Bacon (Bacons Rebellion) . On **May 29, 1677 she was the first** of the tribal leaders to sign the Treaty of Middle Plantation, sometimes called the Treaty of 1677.

   During her thirty years as Chief she worked diligently to maintain peace and unity between the tribes and the colonist. Cockacoeske died in Virginia in 1686. She was succeeded by **Queen Betty** (a niece). She will reign from 1686 until her death in 1708.
   A statue of **Queen Cockacoeske** stands at the Virginia Women's Monument Memorial.

30. Elena Lucrezia Cornaro Piscopia, aka Helen Cornaro, is the first woman to receive a PH.D. degree in 1678 Italy. She was born in Venice on June 5, 1646. She passed away in 1684 of tuberculosis. In 1999 writer Jane Smith Geurnsey wrote the biography of Elena entitled: 'The Lady Cornaro: Pride and Prodigy of Venice'.

wikipedia.org/wiki/Treaty_of_1677, wikipedia.org/wiki/Cockacoeske

31. *1682* - Lawrence C. Wroth published a book called "A History of Printing in Colonial Maryland" 1686-1776. In it he documents **the first licensed female printer as Dinah Nuthead**. She and her husband started a little printing business in Jamestown, Virginia in **1682**. Primarily printing forms for the government, they moved the business to Maryland in **1686**. Her husband, William died in **1695** and so Dinah requested, before an official court, to be named administrator of his estate and asked the Maryland General Assembly that she be granted a license to continue the business of printing government forms. Her request was granted.

32. The first woman, and the first person, to be executed during the Salem Witch Trials was Bridget Bishop on June 10, 1692. She was a sixty-year old mother of three. Five more women were executed on July 19, 1692: Sarah Good (age 39), Rebecca Nurse (71), Susannah Martin (70), Elizabeth Howe (56) and Sarah Wildes (65). In August of 1692 another five were hanged; four men and one woman, Martha Carrier (age 45-ish). Martha's family was the first family to settle Andover, Massachusetts. Eight more hangings took place in September of 1692; one man and seven women: Mary Eastey (58) sister to Rebecca Nurse who was hanged in July. Martha Corey (72) whose husband was also executed after being found guilty of witchcraft. He was pressed to death, while Martha was hanged. Anne Pudeator (71-ish), Mary Parker (55), Alice Parker, Wilmot Redd, Margaret Scott (77).

Some women died in prison waiting for trial or for their execution to be carried out like Ann Foster.

33. On December 28, 1694 Queen Mary II succumbed to smallpox at the age of thirty-two.

1700

34. *December 20, 1700* – Mary Bradbury who successfully escaped prison after being accused and convicted of being a witch in 1692 dies on December 20, 1700, at the age of 85 in what is now Massachusetts. She survived long enough in hiding for the hysteria to be discredited and she was allowed to live out her remaining years without fear. Ray Bradbury is said to be the seventh great grandson of Mary Bradbury, and Ralph Waldo Emerson a fourth great grandson.

I found this piece about Mary Bradbury in a New York Times article in 1879:

"Among the persons thus charged with witchcraft was Mary Bradbury, a woman of 75 years. The wife of one of the most prominent and honorable citizens of the town of Salisbury. She was a woman of exceptionally high standing in Christian life and character. She and her husband had been residents of Salisbury for over 50 years and were the lifelong friends of Robert Pike. Their son, Wymond Bradbury, had married Sarah Pike, eldest daughter of Robert, 30 years before. The families were thus associated by ties of the most intimate character. On the arrest of Mary Bradbury, Robert Pike naturally entered into the case with all the zeal and energy of his nature. If anything was wanting beyond the native impulses of his character to induce him to embark in opposition to the fanatical storm then raging, we have it in this family connection. He was, however, unable to obtain Mary Bradbury's acquittal. She was convicted along with five others, but escaped for some reason now unknown."

1701

35. *May 1701 –* "The Queen has issued out an order to regulate the apparel of ladies, in which there are great alterations. Her majesty is shortly expected here to take upon her the Regency of the Kingdom and in the meantime Cardinal Portocarrero has the sole administration of affairs". ~ **London**

36. *July 22, 1701 –* London: "They write from *Uzez in Languedock that two men have been broken alive upon the wheel in that place upon account of the Protestant religion and a pretended sacrilege, and that two women have received the same punishment for the like occasion **which is the first has been practiced against women** as being contrary to natural modesty." ~ **The Post Man, London, England**

MUSING

AT the Famous Dutch Womans Booth, overagainſt the Hoſpital Gate, during the time of Bartholomew Fair, where 6 Companies of Rope Dancers are joyned in one, they being the greateſt performers of Men, Women and Children, that could be found beyound the Seas, where will be performed ſuch wonderful variety of Dancing, Vaulting. Walking on ehe ſlack Rope, and on the floaping Rope; you will ſee a Wonderful Girle of 10 years of Age, who walks backwards up the floaping Rope, driving a wheelbarrow behind her; alſo you will ſee the Great Italian Maſter, who not only paſſes all that has yet been ſeen upon the low Rope, but he Dances without a pole upon the Head of a Maſt as high as the Booth will permit, and afterwards ſtands upon his Head on the ſame. You will alſo be entertained with the merry Conceits of an Italian Scaramouch, who Dances on the Rope wieh 2 Children and a Dog in a wheel-barrow, and a Duck on his Head.

Post Man newspaper, London, England, Aug 19, 1701

1702

37. *April 23, 1702-* **Margaret Fell Dies.** "(England) Margaret Askew married Judge Thomas Fell, of Marsh Grange, near Dalton in Furness, and became Margaret Fell, mistress of Swarthmoor Hall.

There she lived a most abundant life until her death at age 88 in April of 1702. Margaret, you will recall, wrote 'Women's Speaking Justified' while imprisoned".

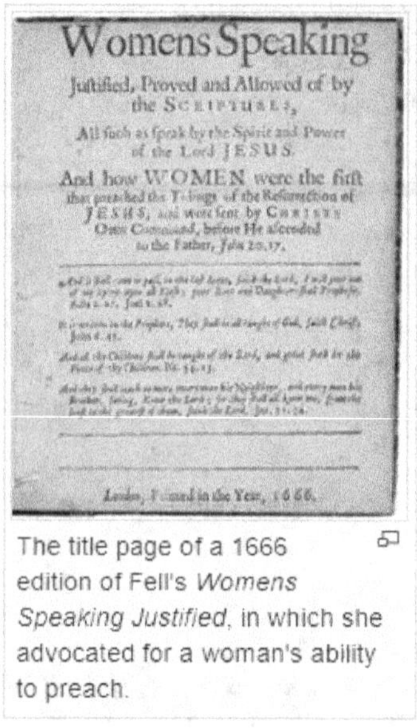

The title page of a 1666 edition of Fell's *Womens Speaking Justified*, in which she advocated for a woman's ability to preach.

Margaret Fell traveled widely over all England when horseback was the only mode, and she left voluminous letters, epistles, tracts and books, [...] **She is considered the mother of Quakerism**. By her hospitality, her writings, her wide correspondence and her wisdom, she not only spread the knowledge of the Quaker interpretation of Christianity, but gave unity and fellowship to a scattered company of men and women of very varied background and experience.

1705

38. In 1705 Maria Sibylla Merian publishes "Metamorphosis Insectorum Surinamensium". Her first book was published in 1675. The first woman (even the first person) to record the details of metamorphosis. Maria was also the first woman to travel to South America on a scientific expedition. Many insects

and plants have been named after her to honor her
extraordinary work.

1708

39. On November 30, 1708 Mary Ball is born in the Colony of
Virginia. She is the mother of President George Washington who
will be born in 1732. For context, Abiah Folger Franklin gave birth
to Benjamin Franklin on January 17, 1706. This means George
Washington's mother Mary and Benjamin Franklin are just two
years apart.

40. Deborah Read is born in 1708 in Birmingham, England. She will
marry Benjamin Franklin in 1730. Some sources say she was
actually born in Philadelphia. According to those who believe she
was born in England show that her family moved to the 'New
World' in 1711 when Deborah was just three years old.

41. Queen Betty, Chief of the Pamunkey Indian Tribe in Virginia dies
in 1708. Not much was known about Queen Betty who became
Chief upon the death of Chief Cockacoeske, also a woman. She is
succeeded by Queen Ann who will continue peace efforts
between the colonist and the Indians during her reign. You can
find a statue of Cockacoeske at the Virginia Capitol as a part of
the Virginia Monument to Women.

1713

42. Susanna Hutchinson Cole, daughter of Anne Hutchinson, passes
away at age 79 in Boston in 1713. She is survived by her three
children.

1715

43. *1715* - It won't be until The U.S. Patent Act of 1790 that women will be allowed to file a patent in their own name here in the United States but, in 1715 Colonial America; meet **Sybilla Righton Masters**. She lays claim to being the **first woman to an invention that was patented in the New World**. She created a 'machine' that produced grits. Previously grinded from corn by hand, her machine automated the process using wooden cylinders, heavy pestles and mortars and powered by the use of horses or water wheels.

    Because the New World was still under British rule the patent was issued by King George of Great Britain making her the **first woman in the English Colony of America to be issued a patent..**

    Sybilla Masters went on to be issued a second patent for a process of making hats and bonnets. This patent was then adapted by others for the use in making baskets, mattings and furniture covers.

1717

44. *January 13, 1717* - **Maria Sibylla Merian** (B1647-D1717), the famous bug lady, dies on January 13, 1717 at the age of 70 in Amsterdam, Netherlands. (refer to #28)

1720

45. Jane Randolph, mother to U.S. President Thomas Jefferson is born on February 10, 1720 in Shadwell, London. Her family moves to Virginia when she was five years old in 1725.

46. July 7, 1720 – Maria Barbara Bach passes away in Germany. She was the first wife of Johann Sebastian Bach. Historians note that Bach was the organist at the church she attended when they met. She and Johann had seven children.

1721

47. December 3, 1721 – Anna Magdalena Bach, a professional singer, becomes the second wife of Johann Sebastian Bach. He and Anna go on to have thirteen children of their own.

1724

48. A newspaper article from The Caledonian Mercury, Scotland, August 17, 1724 – "Modesty Amongst Women. *"This modesty of women has heretofore been look'd upon to be of such consequence to the Welfare of Commonwealths, that wise governments have framed and contrived laws for its preservation, and severely punished offences against it. Thus in the beginning of the Roman Commonwealth, it was death for a woman to drink wine, lest being intoxicated she might betray the modesty of her sex. And a Roman Senator was banished only for having kissed his wife in the presence of his daughter, it being looked upon as a dangerous example of immodesty. The vestal virgins were buried alive, if they violated their vow of chastity and adultery was punished by death."* ~ The Caledonian Mercury, Scotland

1725

49. And this article from the Newcastle Weekly Courant, England dated February 27, 1725 – *"Tis said a new order of the Pope is coming out relating to women's apparel for the future the nobility may be more visibly distinguished from the commoners and that single women more distinguishable from those that are married."* The Newcastle Weekly Courant.

1726

50.   *December 20, 1726* – It is on this date that Hannah Callowhill Penn, widow of William Penn, dies at age fifty-five. She governed the Province of Pennsylvania during her husband's six years of disability following a stroke, and then for another eight years after his death in 1718. Hannah Penn was the first woman to be granted the status of Honorary Citizen of the United States which took an Act of Congress (PL 98-516) and was awarded by President Ronald Reagan in 1984.

MUSINGS

Have you heard of Napkin Nan, aka Nasty Nan, alias Anne Miles?

January 29, 1726 – *"(London): On Friday last, on Anne Miles, alias Napkin Nan, alias Nasty Nan the Scot, was, together with a *char-woman, committed to Newgate by Leonard Street, one of his Majesty's Justices of Peace, for robbing her service the Rose Tavern of a great quantity of napkins, plates, knives, candles, linen and other family necessaries which felonious practice it seems she had carried on in all her places for several years past as appeared by the concession of the char-woman, whose lodging in an alley near Fleet Street was the Waterhouse, or repository for the things stole in that manner and where a great quantity was found upon a search warrant."* ~ The Ipswich Journal, Suffolk, England

> *London, April* 29 Some Days ago a Maiden Lady at Weftminfter, of about 55 Years of Age, and 800 l. a year, made an Offer of Marriage to her Coachman, and directed him to drive for that Purpofe to St. Margaret's Church : But he being ftartled at the Propofal, took her for delirious, and inftantly went for the Apothecary; who judging better, introduced his Son on this critical Occafion, whom fhe accepted and married immediately, to the great Mortification of the honeft Coachman.

The Caledonian Mercury, Edinburgh, Scotland, 1727

"(London) Some days ago a maiden lady at Westminster, of about 55 years of age, and 800 l. a year, made an offer of marriage to her coachman, and directed him to drive for that purpose to St. Margaret's Church. But he being startled at the proposal took her for delirious and instantly went for the apothecary, who judging better, introduced his son on this critical occasion whom she accepted and married immediately, to the great mortification of the honest coachman."

1728

51. As early as 1728 women were working at the post office in Dublin as evident in the following newspaper article dated November 26, 1728: *"(Dublin) We have a melancholy account from Mountmelick, of one Mr. John Moore, an eminent farmer who after two years constant address to Mrs. Crosdale, Postmistress of that place; a widow did some day last week accost the lady in her garden and desired to know if she would consent to marry him. When she absolutely refusing, he pulled out two pistols and discharged them both in his body, upon which he immediately died. Tis observable, both persons are above 50 years old each."* ~ Caledonian Mercury, Edinburgh, Scotland

1729

52. The women have decided to only purchase clothing manufactured in their own community to support their own economy and their local businesses and workers. : *September 25, 1729 – "That 908*

pounds has been collected in and about the city of Dublin for the poor housekeepers and weavers. And that a set of ladies of great fortune have made an agreement among themselves not to wear this winter any cloaths but what should be the produce and manufacture of this Kingdom. And it was not doubted but that so laudable an example will be followed by the rest of the quality, both male and female, by which trade will very probably flourish again and money there once more circulated amongst the public." ~ The Caledonian Mercury, Edinburgh, Scotland, Sept 25, 1729

1731

53. March 6, 1731 Mary Ball marries Augustine Washington. She goes on to have six children. George Washington, the first president of the United States is her first born the following year on February 22, 1732 in Popes Creek, Virginia.

54. June 2, 1731 – First Lady Martha Washington is born Martha Dandridge in Chestnut Grove, Virginia. She is one year older than George Washington.

1732

55. 1732 – *"The first newspaper printed in Rhode Island was at Newport in 1732. James Franklin, a brother to the Doctor (Benjamin Franklin), was the publisher. He died soon after and his widow, Anne Franklin, continued the business several years. She was printer to the colony, supplied blanks to the public offices, published pamphlets and more."* ~ Brooklyn Daily Eagle, New York

A brave woman named Diana. Because this too is a part of women's history. (the letter 'f' was often used as the 's' in type print)

RUN away from her Mafter, a *Muftee* Woman, named Diana, about 20 Years of Age, formerly belonging to Mrs Mary Pike at Goofe Creek: Any Perfon that will bring the Muftee to her Mafter, William Harvey, of Charleftown, fhall be well rewarded.

South Carolina Gazette, Charleston, May 13, 1732

1733

56. *The women protest! March 3, 1733 –* **PROPOSED EXCISE TAX:** *"The humble protest of the ladies in and about the cities of London and Westminster in behalf of themselves, and all the female bodies corporate in Great Britain plainly laying open the many great inconveniencies to which their boroughs in particular will be subject from any further extension of the laws of excise tax.*

We the wives, widows, and spinsters, of London and Westminster and the suburbs thereof being greatly alarmed at the rumor of a general excise tax, intended to be layed on all commodities, beg leave with great humility, to protest. That we shall labor under very great inconveniences and even impossibilities, unless our particulars are accepted." ~ **The Newcastle Newspaper, England**

57. In 1733 we have our first newspaper mention of Cleopatra, that I could find, when two Egyptian mummies, thought to be the bodies of Mark Anthony and Cleopatra were shipped from Cairo by Captain Bookey as a present to the Turkey Company.

December 20, 1733 – **Cleopatra.** "London: There are lately arrived from Turkey by Capt. Bookey, two Egyptian Mummies, said to be the bodies of Mark Anthony and Cleopatra, from Grand Cairo which are accounted very curious having been viewed by several Gentlemen of the Royal Society are to be shown to their majesties and the Royal Family and afterwards to be reposited in Westminster Abbey. They were sent as a present to the Turkey Company." ~ Pennsylvania Gazette, Philadelphia

1735

58. *1735* - The first woman to publish an Almanac, was also the first woman newspaper editor. She is **Anne Franklin**. When her husband, James Franklin (the brother of Benjamin Franklin) passes away in 1732 Ann petitions the General Assembly of Rhode Island to continue the printing business. Her request was granted. She printed books, sermons, advertisements and the five series edition of the Rhode Island Almanac (1737-1741). When Benjamin Franklin published his well-known Poor Richard's Almanac in 1745 Ann began selling that in her shop and by 1758 she began publishing Rhode Island's first newspaper, the Newport Mercury. She would pass away in 1763 at the age of 66.

59. *The Foreign Service was using women to lure men into service.* February 18, 1735 – *"Private letters from Hanover mention that two young women had been lately apprehended there for inveigling the young fellows of several places in that electorate into Foreign Service. The method was for the recruiting officers of a certain neighboring place to plant themselves in ambush near the outskirts of the town and then to detach these girls into the place to look for such young fellows whose height and dexterity rendered them fit for their purpose. These cunning gypsies found means to get familiar with and being of different complexions and both of exquisite beauty were never long at a loss for admirers to whom they always proposed running away together and at the same time making a great show of money and have a wagon at command. Their scheme was easily executed and the men, as soon as the vehicle was arrived in a proper place, were seized by the officers and carried off by force."* ~ Pennsylvania Gazette, Philadelphia

60. Merlin's Cave is a tourist attraction to this day. You may have been!

June 12, 1735 – *"Merlin's Cave, England. A subterraneous work is by her Majesty's order carrying on in the Royal Gardens in Richmond, which is to be called Merlin's Cave, adorned with astronomical figures and characters. Her Majesty was on Monday last to visit it and gave ten guineas among the masons who are employed in executing the design."* ~ The Derby Mercury, Derbyshire, England

A Subterraneous Work is by her Majesty's Order carrying on in the Royal Gardens in Richmond, which is to be called *Merlin's Cave*, adorn'd with Astronomical Figures and Characters: Her Majesty was on Monday last to visit it; and gave ten Guineas among the Masons, &c. who are employ'd in executing the Design.

July 26, 1735 – **A brave woman named Kate**.

Run away from the said *John Whitfield*, a Negro Slave called *Kate*, formerly belonging to *Charles Hart* Esq; whoever brings the same to the said *John Whitfield* at *Dorchester*, or secures her in *Charles-Town* Prison, shall receive *Three Pounds* Reward, besides what the Law directs, by me JOHN WHITFIELD.

The South Carolina Gazette, Charleston

July 26, 1735 - **Mrs. Flavel's shop ad**:

Just imported in the *Mary*, Capt. *Robert Pollixfen* from *London*, and to be sold by *John Johnston* at Mrs. *Flavel's* in Broad-street, a choice parcel of garlix, diapers, gingams, printed callicoes, chillaes, cherriderries, silk and cotton romals, india persians, taffaties, grograms, padusoys,

South Carolina Gazette, Charleston, Jul 26, 1735

1736

61. This headline caught my attention.
    June 24, 1736 – "**Women Taking Up Arms.** *The letters from Petersburg by this post seem to call in doubt what the former had mentioned of the surrender of Asoph and only say, that the Garrison, seeing no hopes of relief, fought like people in despair and* **that the women had taken up arms.** *The famous Count Bonneval is said to command the place.*" ~ Derby Mercury, England

62. 1736 - I would like to introduce you to "**Crazy Sally**". Her given name is Sally Mapps. She moved to Surry about a year ago. A bone-setter by trade; a skill learned from her father who was also a bone-setter. The townspeople describe her as an extraordinary woman and they have contracted with her for another year of service in their community. She is the sister of Polly Peachum.

We hear from Epfom in Surry, that there is lately arrived there a very extraordinary Woman, who calls herſelf *Crazy Sally*, who has perform'd ſome very great Cures in Bone-ſetting, to the Admiration of that Neighbourhood; among the reſt, ſhe ha[illegible] has been quite uſeleſs from the Time of his Birt[illegible] has been offer'd 100 Guineas to continue there a Year. 'Tis ſaid this Woman is Daughter of one War- ren, a Bone-ſetter of Hindon in Wilts, and Siſter to that *Polly Peachum* whom a Gentleman of Fortune marry'd; and that ſhe, upon ſome Family-Quarrel, left her Father, and wander'd about the Country in a miſerable Manner.

August 7, 1736 – "We hear from Epsom in Surry that there is lately arrived a very extraordinary woman who calls herself Crazy Sally who has performed very great cures in bone setting to the advisability of that neighborhood. Among them she has been quite useful. Tis said this woman is daughter of one Warren, a bonesetter of Hindon in Wilts and sister to that Polly Peachum whom a gentleman of fortune married and that she, upon some family quarrel left her father and wondered about the country in a miserable manner." ~ Newcastle Weekly Courant, Tyne and Wear, England

63. We find many instances throughout history where women passed themselves off as men in order to join the military.

   August 19, 1736 – *"They give us an uncommon story from Compaine, that a young woman was come thither to present a petition to the French King, dressed in the Regimentals of a soldier, having served four years as a Grenadier in Bourbon's Regiment of Foot and behaved very gallantly in several actions when at last being discovered by a washer woman she was discharged with an honorable Certificate of her bravery on which she grounded her hopes of some gratuity from the court to enable her to get her future livelihood agreeable to her sex."* **~The Derby Mercury Newspaper, Derbyshire, England**

64. Mrs. Mapps, the bonecutter, continues to perform "extraordinary cures" in her community as related by this article from the Newcastle Weekly Courant date Aug 28, 1736:

On Monday last Mrs. Mapp of Epsom made extraordinary Cures on the Son of Mr. Freeman in Gutter-Lane, and the Daughter of Mr. Nockolls in Cannon-street; and 'tis said there are no less than 50 at present waiting her Operation.——Her new-marry'd Husband hath left her, and carry'd off with him 102 Guineas.

   August 28, 1736 - *"On Monday last Mrs. Mapp of Epsom made extraordinary cures on the son of Mr. Freeman in Gutter Lane and the daughter of Mr. Nockolls in Cannon Street. Tis said there are no less than 50 at present waiting her operation. Her new marry'd husband hath left her, and carr'd off with him 102 Guineas."* ~ **Newcastle Weekly Courant**

   September 7, 1736 - *"Mrs. Mapp continue to surprise every body by her extraordinary operations; she not only cures accidental dislocations, but even rectifies nature, as it happened in the café of a child of 3 years old belonging to Mr. Dirrel, a farmer in Surrey, who was born with the feet turned backward. Though no surgeon would meddle with the said child, yet the doctoress undertook him; immediately settled his limbs in their natural situation insomuch that the young patient is able to walk by the help of bandages, which is more* *than he could ever do before"* ~ Caledonian Mercury, Edinburgh, Scotland

---

Mrs. Sally Mapps was born Sally Wallin in Wiltshire, England, baptized in 1706; her year of death documented as sometime during 1737.

Epsom was the epicenter for the wealthy horse racing community and she often tended to the injured race horses.   She performed some 'noteworthy' operations that were documented in a book by James Caulfield, "Portraits, Memoirs, and Characters of Remarkable Persons" one of which was the surgery to repair the spinal deformity on Sir Hans Sloane's niece.

1737

65. *July 28, 1737 – "Last week a curious fine monument, done by Mr. Rysbrack of Oxford Road was set up in the Church at Kedleston near Derby to the memory of the late Sir Nation Curzon and his lady on which is the following inscription"*
~Derby Mercury, Derbyshire, England

This Monument was erected in Honor of the memory of Sir Nathaniel Curzon and
Dame Sarah Curzon,
his wife
who is the daughter of William Penn.
Sir Nathaniel Curzon on the 4th day of March 1718 and Dame Sarah Curzon, his wife, on the 4th day of January 1727.

66. **Rest In Peace**:

   December 24, 1737 - *"Last week died, at her lodgings near the Seven Dials, the much talked of Mrs. Mapp, the lady bone-setter, so miserably poor, that the parish was obliged to bury her."*

1739

67. (1739) Elizabeth Timothy's husband, who published the South Carolina Gazette newspaper, a contract with Benjamin Franklin, died in 1739. Elizabeth Timothy went to Benjamin Franklin to tell him her desire to continue to print the paper. Mr. Franklin said yes making Elizabeth Timothy, some say, the first woman to publish a newspaper. Perhaps the first in the state of North Carolina.

1740

68. *1740* - Many women were negatively affected by the Negro Act of 1740. Passed in South Carolina it made it illegal for enslaved blacks to raise their own food, earn money, or even learn to write. It also made it legal for 'owners' to kill their slaves without repercussions. The Act spread throughout the South being deemed legal by many State Supreme Courts.

1741

69. In 1741 a woman named Elizabeth Pinckney tries time and time again to create the indigo blue color dye that was very popular at the time. It took three years of trial and error but she did

successfully grow the indigo plant for dye after getting assistance from an African from the West Indies. I was unable to find the name of the man or woman who assisted her in developing the dye. A bit of trivia: Elizabeth Pinckney's son Charles is one of the signers on the United States Constitution. Her son Thomas negotiated the Pinckney's Treaty of 1795 as the Minister to Spain. This gave America navigation right down the Mississippi River.

Elizabeth Pinckney dies of cancer in 1793. It is reported that George Washington was a pall bearer at her funeral.

For her contribution to the agriculture business of South Carolina Elizabeth was the first woman inducted into the South Carolina Business Hall of Fame in 1989. You see, her indigo plant seeds led to a wide expansion of indigo production. The result increased the amount of indigo dye that was exported from 5000 pounds during the years of 1745 and 1746 to a whopping 130,000 pounds by the year 1748! This made indigo second only to rice as South Carolinas cash crop and greatly contributed to the wealth of the planters in that state.

70. In January of 1741 Hannah Waterman Arnold, age 35, gives birth to Benedict Arnold. Hanna, herself, was born in Connecticut in 1706. She dies in 1758 at age 52 in Connecticut.

1743

71. 1743 –

This Week a Female Servant belonging to a Practitioner in the Law near the Royal Exchange died suddenly in her Chair; her Belly being observed to be bigger than usual, she was seen after open'd by a Surgeon, and found to be far gone with Child; 'twas imagined she had taken Medicines to procure Abortion, which was the Cause of her Death,

Mar

ch 26, 1743 - "This week a female servant belonging to a practitioner in the law near the Royal Exchange died suddenly in her chair; her belly being observed to be bigger than usual, she was seen after open'd by a surgeon and found to be far gone with child; twas imagined she had taken medicines to procure abortion, which was the cause of her death." ~ The Ipswich Journal, England

1744

72. Abigail Smith Adams, future First Lady of the United States is born on November 22, 1744 in Weymouth, Massachusetts.

1745

73. *"**Mrs. Anne Franklin** printed for the government an edition of the laws, containing 310 folio pages in 1745. She was aided in her office by her two daughters. They were correct and quick compositors and very sensible women."* ~ Brooklyn Daily Eagle, New York

---

A brave woman, Katherine Russell.

RAN away from the Subscriber, living in *Orange* County, near the Court-house, on the 20th of *June* last, a Servant Woman, named *Katherine Russell*; she is a short, thick, young *Irish* Woman, about 18 Years of Age, of a red Complexion : She had on when she went away, a new brown Linen Petticoat, an old Cotton ditto, and an old Cotton Waistcoat. Whoever will take up the said Servant, and deal with her as the Law directs, so that I may have her again, shall have Thirty Shillings Reward, paid by

John Smith, Jun.

The Virginia Gazette, Oct 24, 1745

1748

74. Potatoes became much more relevant during the middle of the 18th century, proving to be not only a more versatile food but the potato withstood longer periods of storage where other food would rot. A Swedish Countess, **Eva Ekeblad** discovered a process to make alcohol and flour by using potatoes. Eva Ekeblad becomes **the first woman to become a member of the Royal Swedish Academy of Sciences** in **1748**

1750

75. *1750* - **Martha Dandridge**, (the future 'first', First Lady) marries her first husband, Daniel Parke Custis. She is eighteen years old and Daniel is a 38 year old wealthy farmer. Together they have four children of which only two live pass their young childhood.

   Daniel B1751-D1754, died at age 3
   Frances B1753-D1757, died at age 4
   John 'Jacky' Custis B1754-D1781, dies at age 27
   Martha 'Patsy' Custis B1756-D1773, dies at age 17

Her husband Daniel Custis dies the same year as their daughter Frances in 1757. Martha was twenty-five years old. Her son Jacky was three and daughter Patsy was just one. Her husband's death left her a wealthy woman. Martha would marry the future President George Washington just two years later in 1759.

1752

76. *January 1, 1752* - Seamstress who was commissioned to make our U.S. Flag is born on January 1, 1752 in Gloucester City, Colony of New Jersey, British America. Born **Elizabeth Griscom, aka Betsy Ross.**

77. *May 18, 1752* – **Abiah Folger Franklin**, mother of Benjamin Franklin, dies on May 18, 1752 at the age of 84. Her son, Ben Franklin, now in his forties, was the president of the College of Philadelphia (now University of Pennsylvania) and was Postmaster of Philadelphia at the time of his mother's death.

1753

78. *May 8, 1753* - Poetess Phillis Wheatley is born on May 8, 1753 in West Africa.

79. Mother Goose is thought to have been written as far back as the 1600s and some theories trace the origin of the Mother Goose fairytale as being based on the biblical Queen of Sheba.

In the United States popular theory is that the original Mother Goose was based on the wife of Isaac Goose, **Mary Goose** who lived from

1657-1690 and with ten children was known as "Mother Goose". **You can even visit her grave in Boston, Massachusetts.**

According to this 1753 article below the tales have a French origin, *"these tales are dedicated to a princess of the blood of France"*. "Written as encouragement of virtue". In French by Perrault and in English by R.S. Gent.

August 31, 1753 – "The fourth edition, beautifully printed of Mother Goose's Tales. Being histories and tales of past times

*with morals. Written in French by M. Perrault, and English by R. S. Gent. These tales are dedicated to a real **Princess of France**, and the famous Perrault was so taken with her that he made himself their morals, as knowing they intended to the encouragement of virtue, and depressing of vice; the true end and design of the fable."* ~ Derby Mercury, England

1754

80. In 1754 The Pennsylvania Gazette printed the following excerpt from 'The Female Advocate'. This gives us a sense of the attitudes about women in 1754 and how they were viewed in society. *June 20, 1754* — Excerpt from 'The Female Advocate': *"People have been extremely divided in their opinions about the fair sex and there is hardly any country where their usage doth not run to an extreme, that is, they are either very highly valued or else very grossly abused. Man, who had the right of eldership in the creation immediately made use of the authority which seemed to be given him in Genesis and took the opinion that the earth is given to the male sex for an inheritance, prevailed so far, that in the east they have ever styled the men their Lords and masters. The Jews, who are the most ancient nation in the world invented certain marks of servitude to keep their women in submission, and even among their finest ornaments, mixed tokens of a pompous slavery. Hence arose the chains and bracelets, and the boring their ears, which was common to women and slaves, and however ornamental the dress of that sex might be, men always disdained to wear it as being the distinction of an inferior creature. The common opinion then being, that men were made to command. Some have been so very kind to themselves as to believe that women were associated with men only to obey them, and thereupon have assumed as despotic and arbitrary a power over them as over any of the mute creation.*

But upon an impartial examination we shall find but little room for this unlimited superiority and that there are but very few points in which the ladies seem to be any ways inferior. Women have been known to excel in politics and the art of government, and their government has been many times preferable to that of the men. In science several have arrived at the highest perfection, but above all, it is to them we are indebted for the politeness, neatness, and engaging behavior which constitute the pleasures of a civil life. Their manners are most gentle, their voice and way of speaking more musical and entertaining, and, in short, they have a certain excellence which nature has given them peculiar to themselves, which men may at a distance admire, but must never pretend to imitate.

The enemies of the sex will search even the scriptures for frightful descriptions of women, and will, I don't doubt, charge me with partiality but I insist upon it, that I do but bare justice. I don't pretend to say that women have fewer faults than men. No, we are equally the children of the fist unhappy pair, but I can't see why the errors of the women should shock us more than our own, unless it is, that we entertain an opinion that they ought to be better than ourselves. We are apt to resent it when we see them deviate from what we think their duty at the same time that we are apt to indulge ourselves in more heinous transgressions, whereas the obligation is mutual and equal and the distribution of distinct offices to each sex is necessary to keep the world in order. Men must attend the affairs of a social life, as well as the women those of a domestic one, and the latter are as praise worthy and as much to be respected for their female excellencies, as the former for those that are more manly.

The ancient Romans were of this opinion; and masters as they were of all the politeness and power in the world, acknowledged their females to be their other half. This distinguishing indulgence caused a noble emulation in the ladies, as they were used better to behave better than their neighbors in proportion and as their privileges excelled those of other nations so did their honor, wisdom and virtue.

How brutish then are those men who use them ill, defenseless as they are against violence? Nor is it less harmful to insult them for the use of those arts, which the ill practices of men make necessary for them. We tax them with being cunning, malicious, inconsistent and above all, incapable of keeping a secret while at the same time we make a boast of our own infidelity and treachery. Is there anything more indiscreet than a fop, or more vain and scandalous than the common discourses of young fellows. A woman never talks of the faults she has committed unless the falsehood of her seducer forces her to it. Whereas, without the least provocation, it is common for men to boast of favors. Nay, very often of those they never received.

Besides, the women are often blamed for actions by the very persons who solicited them to the commission of them, who, devil like, first tempt, and then insult them with weaknesses that themselves only occasioned. This is the very reverse of good sense and honesty but nothing more common and it is to be wished that there were some very severe penalty inflicted by law, in cases of this nature, which, if it did not wholly suppress the actions, would at least suppress the publishing them and consequently prevent abundance of very influencing ill examples.

This puts me in mind of the answer of a great wit of the last age, when the plan of a bill to be brought into parliament was showed him for his approbation; the title was, 'A bill for the better preventing the heinous sins of adultery and fornication; the penalty to the convicted transgressor of either sex was death.' His Grace said, it was a good wholesome bill but he was of opinion that the title might be mended that instead of 'for the better preventing the heinous sins of adultery and fornication' it ought to be 'for the better concealing them'. Intimating that the severity of the penalty would only occasion more secrecy, but if it did that, I humbly conceive it would do a great deal.

If it be objected, that women are warned to guard the first approaches and prudently in this case, like the Adder, turn a deaf ear to the charmer, charm he ever so sweetly. In answer to this it ought to be considered how artful men are in their attacks and how imperceptibly they insinuate themselves into the lady's good graces, how ready they are to take all advantages of their ignorance, innocence, or curiosity. The first woman had, no doubt, more knowledge and fortitude than any of her posterity yet the cunning of the tempter prevailed and engaged her in an action which entailed misery and imperfection on all her issue.

Upon the whole, it may very justly be concluded that women have at least equal excellencies with the men and if any time they are guilty either of any vices or weaknesses it is generally *owing, either to masculine provocations or temptations. I could add a great deal more on this head, but that may engage me to correspond with you hereafter, who am, your humble servant, - Philander."* ~ The Pennsylvania Gazette, Philadelphia

1755

81. **November 2, 1755** Maria Antonia Josepha Johanna is born. We all know her as Marie Antoinette.

82. *November 8, 1755 – "The Assembly of Virginia having lately laid on a kind of poll tax, a list of those liable has been made out, by which it appears that there are 43,443 whites, 60,755 blacks, liable in this tax.* **No white women pay**, *and the men only from sixteen to sixty;* **but the black women all pay.***"*

1756

83. **Lydia Taft**. First woman to legally vote in colonial America on October 30, 1756 in Uxbridge, Massachusetts. Although women were not legally permitted to cast a vote, the people of Uxbridge agreed she could vote as the widow and executor of her late husband's estate since her husband's only other male relative, his brother, was underage.

1758

84. In November of 1758 Halley's comet is predicted to be next year on April 13, 1759 **by Nicole Reine Lepaute, a woman**, along with colleague Alexis Clairaut, a man. **The first time a successful prediction has been made by astronomers, one being a female, of the return of a comet.**

85. Elizabeth Carter wrote the first English translation of the Discourses of Epictetus in 1758. Elizabeth Carter [id90] dies on February 19, 1806 at age 88.

ALL the Works of EPICTETUS, which are now extant; confisting of his Difcourfes, preferved by ARRIAN. In Four Books. The Enchiridion and Fragments. Tranflated from the original Greek by ELIZABETH CARTER. With an Introduction and Notes, by the Tranflator.

Public Advertiser, London, England, April 17, 1758

April 17, 1758 – "All the works of EPICTETUS which are now extant consisting of his discourses preserved by Arrian in four books, the Enchiridion and Fragments. Translated from the original Greek by Elizabeth Carter. With an introduction and notes by the translator." ~Public Advertiser, England

1759

86. January 6, 1759 - A twenty-seven year old Martha Custis marries twenty-six year old George Washington at the St. Peters Church in New Kent County, Virginia. She wore purple silk shoes on her wedding day that are now on display at the Mount Vernon Museum.

On Jan. 6, 1759, at St. Peter's Church, New Kent county, Virginia, the Rev. John Mossum performing the ceremony.

The following is an account of how George and Martha met: [...] *"Washington was on his way to Williamsburg when he met Mr. Chamberlayne, and according to Virginia custom one must pay homage at the fireside of hospitality and obliged visiting for a time and met there, in Mr. Chamberlayne's mansion a beautiful Mrs. Martha Custis." [...] "before me I have an original picture of Mrs. Washington. She represents a figure rather below the middle size, with hazel eyes and hair of the same color, finely rounded arms, a beautiful chest and taper waist dressed in a blue silk robe of the fashion of the times."*

87. A newspaper article about women joining the secretive Free Masons: *March 7, 1759 – "For Female Satisfaction. Whereas the mystery of Free Masonry hath been kept a profound secret for several ages, till at length some men assembled themselves at the Dover Castle in the Parish of Lambeth, under pretense of knowing the secrets, and likewise in opposition to some gentlemen that are real free masons and hold a lodge at the same house; therefore, to prove that they are no more than pretenders, and as the ladies have sometimes been desirous of gaining knowledge of the noble art, several regular made masons (both ancient and modern) members of constituted lodges in this metropolis, have thought proper to unite into a select body, at Beau Silvesters, the sign of the angel, Bull-Stairs, Southwark, and style themselves unions, think it highly expedient, and in justice to the fair sex, to initiate them therein provided they are women of undeniable character; for tho' no lodge as yet, except the Free Union Masons, have though proper to admit women into their fraternity, we, well knowing they have as much right to attain to the secrets as those Castle Humbugs, have thought proper so to do, not doubting but they will prove an honor to the craft; and as we have had the honor to inculcate ourselves capable of having the secret conferred on the, by proper application will be admitted and the charges will not exceed defraying the expenses of our lodge."* ~ The Public Advertiser, London, England

88. **1759 - As predicted** (see item #84), Halley's Comet was spotted in the skies. The Pennsylvania Gazette printed this article on April 19th:

Cambridge, April 7, 1759

~ The Comet, which has for some time been a pretty general topic of conver-
sations and the prediction of which has excited curiosity in many and terror in
more has at length, tho within the time prefixed, made its appearance."

newspapers.com/clip/63915080/halleys-comet-1759/

89. August 15, 1759 - Hannah W. K. Arnold, mother of Benedict
Arnold dies on **August 15, 1759**. Benedict would have been 18
years old at the time. Her son, Benedict Arnold dies on **June 14,
1801**

*Benedict has a sister named Hannah Arnold, named after her
mother. **Sister Hannah manages the pharmacy Benedict had
opened in 1762 in New Haven, Connecticut.**

1760

February 16, 1760 – "To The Publick. The influence of woman over the heart of man is such, that every improvement of her perfection must be an addition to his happiness.

To preserve this influence should be her first care: But as prejudice seems at present to mistake its foundation and limit it to the external beauties of the form, whose power, mighty as it is, soon fails, if unsupported by the virtues of the mind, this undertaking is designed to raise her attention to the real excellency of her nature, and awaken her from the listless dissidence and intoxication, in which she has been so long lulled by flattery and neglect.

Your most devoted servant, Charles Honeycombe." ~ **Newcastle Weekly Courant**

1761

90. *1761* – Writer Phillis Wheatley is kidnapped from West Africa, in 1761 at age 8, and brought to the Americas to be sold into slavery.

1763

MUSINGS of 1763

A Perſon Died lately, who left a large Eſtate to a Female Relation, provided ſhe would Marry one of the Name of Pearce. She not knowing any one of that Name, advertiſed in the public Papers, That if any ſuch Perſon would come to her, he might hear of ſomething to his Advantage. At Length one came, to whom ſhe would give 150 l. per Annum, if he would Marry her, ſettle the Reſt of her Fortune upon her, and live elſewhere. Which Propoſal he gladly accepted, being juſt releaſed from Jail by the Inſolvent-Act.

Maryland Gazette, Annapolis, MD Jan 13, 1763

1766

91. *October 9, 1766 –* (Albany) *"On Saturday night last four Indian Chiefs, three Indian women, and two interpreters, arrived in town. It is said their business here is to complain against some Dutch settlers near Albany for encroaching on their lands and driving them from their plantations which encroachments are represented to contain 400 square miles or thereabouts.*

   Orders are given for the Indian Chiefs and women, just arrived in town from America, to be supported at the government's expense, during their stay here." ~ The Pennsylvania Gazette, Philadelphia, PA

WHEREAS I the Subscriber did some Time ago falsly, maliciously and scandalously speak, report, utter, and publish, in the Hearing of Joseph Edmanson, and other Persons, in the Parish of St. Paul, that a certain young Woman in the said Parish named Martha Stevens was big with Child. I do hereby declare that I have no Ground or Reason to defame the said Martha Stevens, but do believe her to be a virtuous, honest, young Woman, and that I did utter the said Words in a wanton Manner, and own that I am a Liar. Given from under my Hand this 11th Day of April, 1766.   CHRISTOPHER HILL.
Witness, BENJAMIN STEVENS, JOHN EDMANSON, jun.

South Carolina Gazette, Charleston, Apr 29, 1766

1767

92. ***May 8, 1767*** – *"**Anne Katharine Greene**, was born in Holland. In 1767 she succeeded her husband in publishing the Maryland Gazette, the first paper printed in that state. She executed the Colony printing and continued the business to her death in 1775."*
~ Brooklyn Daily Eagle, Brooklyn, New York

93.   The message here is that the ladies of the town have agreed to shop local as to help the local manufacturers. ***November 19, 1767*** - *"In a large circle of very agreeable ladies in this town, it was unanimously agreed to lay aside the use of ribbons for which there has been so great a resort to milliners, in times past. It is hoped that this resolution will be followed by others of the sex, throughout the province. How agreeable will they appear in their native beauty, stripped of these ornaments from the prevailing motive of love to their country.*
We must, after all our efforts, depend greatly upon the female sex for the introduction of O-economy amongst us: and those who have the pleasure of an acquaintance with them, assure us, that their utmost aid will not be wanting.
So strong I the disposition of the inhabitants of this town to take off the manufactures that come from the country, towns,

especially women's and children's winter apparel, that nothing is wanting but an advertisement, where they may be had in town, which will be taken in, and published by the printers of the Boston Gazette, gratis." ~ Maryland Gazette, Annapolis, MD

1768

94. *1768* - Nine year old Nannette Stein, the daughter of piano maker J.A. Stein practiced her piano under the expert care of her father. The piano was invented in 1700. Its predecessor was an instrument called the harpsichord. The piano was considered the harpsichord improved! Very expensive, only for the wealthy, mostly the Royals at the time, and in fact was not played in public until 1768 when Johann Christian Bach was convinced to do so. Wealthy women and their daughters were being taught to play the piano but only in the home. Not for public concerts like the men were allowed.

95. ***July 25, 1768*** - Lydia Hill postmaster of the Boston Post office has died.

Boston Evening Post, July 25, 1768.

Last Thursday died at Salem, Mrs. *Lydia Hill,* who for many years kept the Post-Office.

Boston Evening Post, August 1, 1768.

1769

96. **1769 - Margery Minnikin.** What I can surmise of the following 'Letter To The Editor' from Miss Minnikin is that she is 'making light' that the men currently serving in these positions of government are no more qualified than the women she has named. I found it amusing, if not brave, of her, to be so bold at a time when a woman's opinion was not appreciated and women

were encouraged to keep quiet; not speak out. I also applaud the newspaper for printing it!

***November 7, 1769* – Letter To The Editor.** *"I must give inexpressible concern to a person who feels for the distresses of his country, to peruse the descriptions daily exhibited of our decline in power, virtue, industry, and every good quality for which we were formerly distinguished among the first nations in the world. One writer ascribes it to the general system of corruption which has been gaining ground for a succession of ages. Another places it to the account of a too numerous and still increasing aristocracy interfering with elections, a measure that must, one day or other, destroy the balance of our constitution, while a third, with equal reason, lays it down as an invariable rule, that nothing great or praise-worthy can be effected by a ministry whose principal attention must be devoted to their own safety, amidst the hurry and clamor of popular remonstrance and general dissatisfaction.*

It is universally allowed, that the King, who is the common parent of his people, has exhausted every measure which the most consummate prudence could suggest for the good of his subjects and this appears in nothing more conspicuously, than the frequent changes which have been made in the higher departments of government to how little purpose the public, alas, are already too well acquainted.

I have been for some time past a silent observer of public measures with the reasons given by writers on both sides for that clamor which both ins and outs begin to think are risen to a dangerous pitch and by your leave, my good masters, you are all mistaken. I have penetrated the true cause and will boldly affirm what may be proved upon principles of found philosophy that the fault does not lie in the hearts, but the heads of the Lords of the creation. In plain terms, the powers of the men are the worse for wear and must be permitted to lie sallow till such time as they are judged capable of reassuming their places, with reputation to themselves and advantage to the nation. In the meantime, I most dutifully and humbly beg that his Majesty would listen to the entreaties of many of his faithful subjects, and graciously appoint:

WOMENS HISTORY TRIVIA

Mrs. Macaulay, First Lady of the Treasury because she despises money and has a sufficient resource in her own genius.

Mrs. Lenox and Mrs. Brookes, Secretaries of State. It is presumed they will be as careful of national secrets as they have been of their own.

The Dutchess of K--, Mistress of the horse, as her grace is already familiar with the whole mystery of the manege.

Lady Harr--, Chancellor of the Exchequer, a lady every way capable of opening the budget.

The Dutchess of N- -, First Lady of the Admiralty on account of her being a skillful navigator.

Miss Parsons, one of the Ladies of Trade, she already having had great experience in commerce.

The Dutchess of B- - , President of the Council, and Matchmaker general to the nation.

Miss Williams, to command the Gentlemen Pensioners, having long directed the motions of Dr. Johnson.

Miss Carter, to be Historiographer General and record the achievements of the whole group.

I have ventured to select a few from the many who are unexceptionably qualified to serve their country and have only to add, that if this hint is thought worthy of attention, the ale part of his Majesty's subjects will have time to renovate their languid and exhausted faculties. The consequences must prove salutary and beneficial to a public, sufficiently tired with the frequent and expensive changes of administration. All I desire in return is, that my sister should be appointed mistress of the ceremonies and myself usher of the Black Rod. You will please to observe that it is unnecessary to propose an alteration in the Bench of __, they being generally reckoned old women; and I need not mention how dangerous it is to propose a reformation amongst the sages of the law. {Yours, Margery Minnikin}" ~ The Leeds Intelligencer, Yorkshire, England

1770

97. In **1770** a ladies magazine called "The Lady's Magazine" was started in England. While it was published by a man many of the contributors were women. Mary Russell Mitford among them. 'The Lady's Magazine" set the tone for the future of women's magazine that we have enjoyed for decades.

    The magazine included stories and poems, sheets of music, the latest fashion news, as well as worldly *'news'*. I quote the news because the ladies magazines often presented the same news story quite differently than the men's magazines. As an example, leading up to the French Revolutionary War the men's magazines warned that "Europe is at the present moment in a state of alarm and danger". While the women's magazine reported the Revolutionary war quite differently stating there was no need for worry as the French were no match for the British Navy. Supposedly this was done in an effort not to worry the more fair sex but can you imagine why the husbands argued that their wives didn't understand the ways of the world and how serious certain current events.

1771

98. Women advertised their businesses in the newspaper, as evident here in 1771 **October 17, 1771** – *"I beg leave to acquaint the public that I have opened a Tavern in the house, the other side of the capitol, lately occupied by Mrs. Vohe where those gentlemen who please to favor me with their custom may depend upon genteel accommodations and the very best entertainment.*

I shall reserve rooms for the gentlemen who formerly lodged with me. – Christiana Campbell." ~ Rind's Virginia Gazette, Williamsburg

I BEG leave to acquaint the public that I have opened TAVERN in the house, the other side of the capitol, lately occupied by Mrs. Vobe; where those Gentlemen who please to favour me with their custom may depend upon genteel accommodations, and the very best entertainment.

⁎⁎ I shall reserve rooms for the Gentlemen who formerly lodged with me. CHRISTIANA CAMPBELL.

Rind's Virginia Gazette, Williamsburg, Oct 17, 1771

99. **1771** – *"Penelope Russel has succeeded her husband in printing the 'Censor' at Boston. She is a very industrious and active woman. She not only sets type, but while at her case invokes her muse and puts up type on tragical events in an interesting manner without any written copy."* ~ Brooklyn Daily Eagle, New York

1772

100. *March 12, 1772* – Woman Posing as Soldier. *"(Paris) There is a girl now upon our theatre who is about twenty one years of age, seven of which she served in the Regiment of Belsunce, France. She killed one of her comrades in a duel, which affair she got the better of, but in a quarrel since she was wounded herself, which occasioned the discovery of her sex. She has been presented at court and it is said has had a small place given her in the King's stables."* ~ The Virginia Gazette, Williamsburg

London, Leeds, Wakefield, Barnsley, Shef-
field, and Mansfield

FLYING MACHINE,

In TWO DAYS for the SUMMER SEASON,
SETS out from Mrs. COOKE's, the
Old-King's-Arms, Leeds, every Monday, Wednesday, and Friday at Two o'Clock in the Morning; and
from the Swan-with-Two-Necks, Lad-Lane, London,
every Night as usual; meets and lies at Nottingham both
up and down.   £. S. D.
Each Inside Passenger from Leeds and Wake-
    field to London
Outside from Ditto to Ditto
Each Inside Passenger allowed 14lb. Weight of Luggage,
and Outside ditto 7lb. all above to pay.
        Perform'd (if God permit) by
    HANFORTH and MOUNTAIN, London.
    T. HILLYARD, Dunstable.
    J. BENTON, Harbro'.
    J. FOSTER, Loughbro',
    W. SIMES, Mansfield.
    J. OWEN, Sheffield.
    Passengers and Parcels entered at Jeremiah Cooke's,
opposite the Back-Way to the Old-King's-Arms,
and at J. Bleasby's, at the Talbot-Inn, Wakefield.
    The Proprietors will not be answerable for Writ-
ings, Jewels, Plate, Cash, &c. except entered as such,
and paid for accordingly.

The Leeds Intelligencer and Yorkshire General Advertiser, Leeds, West Yorkshire, England June 23, 1772

The first 'hot air balloon' is said to have taken place in 1783 but it was certainly not the first time humans rose above the ground. Mrs. Cooke has a set schedule, prices and weight of luggage limits all listed in the above ad from 1772 London.

1773

101. **1773** - Martha Washington's daughter Martha 'Patsy' Custis dies at age 17 from an epileptic seizure.

102.   **1773** – *"Mrs. Elizabeth Timothy, after the death of her husband in 1773 continued publishing the Gazette in Charleston. She continued its publication a few years, until she was succeeded by her son. Anne Timothy, the widow of this son, after the revolutionary war, revived the Gazette which had been discontinued while the British troops were in possession of Charleston. She was appointed printer to the state and held the office until 1792."* ~ **Brooklyn Daily Eagle, New York**

103.   May 29, 1773 – *"Published: Whimsical Anecdotes of the celebrated Signora Gabrieli, **the first woman singer in Europe**."* ~ Jackson's Oxford Journal, Oxfordshire, England

104.   *June 17, 1773 – "A few days since an apothecary in Southwark was served with a Judge's warrant for administering certain drugs to a female patient, in order to procure abortion."* ~Rind's Virginia Gazette, Williamsburg

A few days since an apothecary in Southwark was served with a Judge's warrant for administering certain drugs to a female patient, in order to procure abortion.

Rind's Virginia Gazette, VA Jun 17, 1773

105. **1773** – Phillis Wheatley became the first black woman to publish a book when her book of poetry, *'Poems on Various Subjects, Religious and Moral'* was published.

106. July 10, 1773 – (Boston Newspaper) *"Phillis, the extraordinary negro girl here, who is a servant to Mr. John Wheatley of this place, sailed last Saturday for London, under the protection of Mr. Nathaniel Wheatley; since which the following little piece of her's has been published here:*

FAREWELL TO AMERICA

'Addressed to Mrs. Susanna Wheatley' by Phillis Wheatley'

"Adieu New England's smiling meads,
Adieu the flowery plain,
I leave thy opening charms, O spring,
And tempt the roaring main.

In vain for me the flowerets rise and show their gaudy pride,
While here beneath the northern skies I mourn for health denied.

Thee, charming maid while I pursue in thy luxurious reign.
And sigh and languish, thee to view,
Thy pleasures to regain.

Susanna mourns, nor can I bear,
To see the crystal showers
Or mark the tender falling tear
At sad departures hour

Not unregarding can I see
Her soul with grief opprest
But let no sighs, no groans for me,
Steal from her pensive breast.

In vain the feathered warblers sing,
In vain the garden blooms,
And on the bosom of the spring
Breathes out her sweet perfumes.

While for Britannia's distant shore
We sweep the liquid plain,
And with astonish'd eyes explore
The wide extended main.

Lo! Health appears, celestial dame.
Complacent and serene,
With Hebe's mantle over her frame,
With soul delighting main.

To mark the vale where London lies,
With misty vapors crowned
Which cloud Aurora's thousand dyes,
And veil her charms around.

Why, Phoebus, moves thy car so slow?
So slow thy rising ray?
Give us the famous town to view,
Thou glorious king of day!

For thee, Britannia, I resign
New England's smiling fields;
To view again her charms divine,
What joy the prospect yields!

But thou temptation hence away,
With all thy fatal train,
Nor once seduce my soul away,
By thine enchanting strain.

Thrice happy they, whose heav'nly shield
Secures their souls from harms,
And fell temptation on the field
Of all its power disarms."

1774

1774 -   President Thomas Jefferson's grandmother on his mother side. His mother was Jane Randolph Jefferson.

humanity and indulgence.
A few days ago died, Mrs. JANE RANDOLPH, spouse of Thomas Isham Randolph, Esquire, of Chesterfield.

Rind's Virginia Gazette, Williamsburg, Feb 17, 1774

107.   Marie Antoinette is crowned Queen of France on May 10, 1774

108.   *July 1, 1774 – "A letter from Paris asserts positively the pregnancy of the Queen of France."* ~ The Derby Mercury, England

109.   In August of 1774 a letter, addressing the women of Pennsylvania and another in a South Carolina newspaper was printed in response to the Boston Tea Party, December of 1773. I just want to give a brief summary of what the Boston Tea Party was and then the letter posted in the newspapers of how the women responded.

In December of 1773 we experienced the Boston Tea Party protest by the Sons of Liberty in Boston, Massachusetts. The reason for the protest was the Tea Act of May 10, 1773 which allowed the British based company, East India Tea Co. to sell tea from China in the American colonies without paying any taxes. The protesters destroyed shipments of tea sent by the East India Company by boarding the ships and throwing the tea overboard into the Boston Harbor. The British government's response was swift, resulting in the Intolerable Acts of 1774. The Intolerable Acts, legislated by British parliament to punish the protesters and colonists of Massachusetts for their protest of the tea took away the self-governing rights that the colonist of Massachusetts hoping this would deter the remaining of the thirteen colonies from any future revolts.

The initial response of the colonies was to form the First Continental Congress.

Women responded in their own ways; writing articles for the newspaper and organizing anti-tea parties in their communities.

August 29, 1774 – *"To the Ladies of Pennsylvania. Dear Ladies, United as we are by interest and affection, we flatter ourselves we need make no apologies for addressing you on this occasion; so far from thinking them necessary, we doubt not you will receive, as a sisterly freedom the liberty we take in communicating our sentiments to you. Give us leave, in the first place, to condole with you on the unhappy change that a few past years have produced on this extensive continent; our political hemisphere, which, till of late, we have always beheld serenely bright, is now full of clouds that we much fear will burst in tempest over our heads. We propose not, ladies, to enter into the much agitated subject of American grievances. You will undoubtedly hear too much for your peace of mind.*

Your husbands, your fathers, and all your dearest friends of the other sex, have, no doubt, frequently discussed in your presence this momentous point; on the determinations of such friends, we may all safely rely. Let us then, dear ladies, co-operate with them in their hones endeavors to extricate America from the evils that threaten her. Much, very much, depends on the public virtue the ladies will exert at this critical juncture. Permit us, therefore, to exhort you, to be firm in withstanding luxuries of every kind, but above all, as the most pernicious of all, that you will, as we have all universally done, banish India Tea from your tables, and instead substitute some of those aromatic herbs with which our fruitful soil abounds.

We mean not to boast of the conduct of the Virginians in this arduous trial; they know they do nothing more than their indispensable duty, in the sacrifices they have made, and are farther willing to make. Neither do we doubt the good ladies of Pennsylvania will go as far in promoting the general happiness as our country women, or even the steady matrons of Rome ever went for the public good; in short, we have the fullest dependence that the fair-sex of Pennsylvania, Virginia, and of all America, will be so far instrumental in bringing about a redress of the evils complained of, that history may be, hereafter filled with their praises and teach posterity to venerate their virtues. We have the honor to subscribe ourselves, your affectional country women of Virginia." ~ **The Pennsylvania Packet**

Aug 29, 1774, *"South Carolina Gazette, To my sisters and country women: "At a time when the scourge is held up not over this country only, but all America and one of our sister colonies now suffering under the iron hand of power, in the general cause of American liberty and that for a matter which chiefly respects our sex. Surely, my sisters, we cannot be tame spectators when so much remains with us to do and may be reasonably expected of us. By our persisting hitherto in the use of the East India Tea we have opposed our friends, and assisted the enemies of America, to enslave ourselves and posterity. Let us now make it evident to the world that we have some regard for our country and our offspring by joining cheerfully under the faith of a promise to each other to forego the use of all foreign tea as also every kind of East India goods; we shall thereby disappoint our enemies who no doubt build much on our weakness in this respect and greatly assist our husbands, brethren and countrymen in this their arduous struggle. I am credibly informed that many respectable families in this town have already set the laudable example. Every mistress of a family may prohibit the use of tea and East India goods in her family and among her children: under the present circumstances every article from thence is replete with poison and should be rejected with scorn. No longer let our vanity,* *ambition and pride work in opposition to our countrymen now laboring to procure us the free enjoyment of the fruits of their industry. But let us rather strengthen their hands by a hearty concurrence with the. We no longer have any confidence in the British Parliament. We have nothing now to hope from that unholy inquisition but cruelty and injustice. By one act they rob us of our property, and by another of our lives. The constitution must indeed be at the last gasp when those who should be the guardians and protectors of the rights and liberties of the people throughout the wide extended dominions of Great Britain so shamefully betray their trust and barter the lives and fortunes of their fellow subjects for places of profit."* ~ A planters wife.

110. Penelope Barker organized the **first** documented women's political demonstration in the United States when, in 1774 she gathered about fifty fellow women who all signed a resolution to boycott tea.

111. This was a short piece in the newspapers in 1774: ***November 2, 1774 – Marie Antoinette.*** *"The pregnancy of the Queen of France has already been announced, and has been received with the utmost throughout that kingdom. She is universally beloved, which is not to be wondered at; for she gives an excellent example to every lady."*

112. *December 19, 1774 -* Deborah Read Franklin, (1708-1774) wife of Benjamin Franklin dies. She was 66 years old. Her son Francis died years earlier in 1736 at age four. She is survived by her husband Benjamin Franklin and their daughter Sarah. Benjamin passes away in 1790 at the age of 84 and their daughter Sarah Franklin Bache dies in 1808 at age 65.
    The story of how Deborah and Benjamin met is quite funny. As a seventeen year old young man Benjamin was on his way to a local printers to apply for a job. Hungry but unfamiliar with the area bakers he stopped and asked for what he thought would be three small biscuits. What he received was three large loaves of bread. With his large loaves of bread in tow; one under each armpit and one in hand consuming it he continued on his way. As he walked down Chestnut Street he noticed a young woman, Deborah, standing in her doorway watching those passing by. She must have been amused as Benjamin describes the moment in his autobiography as he must have "made a very fantastical appearance" before her.

December 28, 1774 – "On Monday, the 19th, died, in an advanced age, ***Mrs. Deborah Franklin, wife of Dr. Benjamin Franklin.*** *The Thursday following her remains were interred in Christ Church burying ground."* ~ The Pennsylvania Gazette, Philadelphia

1775

113.   Mary Catharine Goddard (B1738-D1816) a postmaster in 1775 and then as the publisher of a newspaper Mary Katharine was just the second newspaper to publish the Declaration of Independence but her copy in the Goddard Broadside, was specifically commissioned by Congress in 1777 as the first newspaper to include the names of all of the men who signed it.

From the Maryland Journal *and* Baltimore Advertiser, *published by* Mary C. Goddard, *August* 14, 1775.

Mary Catharine Goddard was also Postmaster of the Baltimore Post Office from 1775-1789.

114.   *April 3, 1775 –* Minutes of Chester County Committee: Freedom for Black Infants. *"On motion, ordered, that Mr. Hockley, Mr. Johnston, Mr. Gronow, Mr. Lloyd, Mr. Frazer, Mr. Moore, and Mr. Taylor, be, and they are hereby appointed a committee to essay a petition to present to the General Assembly of this province, with regard to the manumission of slaves, especially relating to the freedom of infants hereafter born of black women, within this colony, and do make report of the same to this committee at their next meeting."* ~ The Pennsylvania Packet, Philadelphia
*manumission: release from slavery

115.   *August 11, 1775 – "**Mary Stevens** begs leave to inform the public that in order to enable her to support her family in these hard times she intends retailing at a store in Longitude Lane,*

Madeira Wine by the dozen, Rum of all sorts in any quantity, gin, brandy, coffee, spermacori candles, and many other articles.

She likewise begs leave to express her most grateful acknowledgements to the gentlemen who have frequented her house, and would esteem it an additional favor if such as are indebted to her, would be kind enough to discharge their respective accounts, in order to enable her to satisfy her very urgent creditors." ~ South Carolina Gazette

116.   *September 21, 1775 –* **Sarah Hallam** *"The subscriber begs leave to inform the public that she intends to open a dancing school on Friday the 25ᵗʰ for young ladies. She therefore hopes the gentlemen and ladies will be kind enough to favor her with their daughters. She flatters herself she shall be able to give entire satisfaction as no care or pains on her part will be wanting. Her days for teaching are Friday and Saturday. The price, twenty shillings entrance and four pounds a year. Sarah Hallam Instructor."* ~ Rinds Virginia Gazette, Williamsburg

117.   *November 13, 1775 – "To the good women of this province: As the spinning of yarn is a great part of the business in cloth manufactories, in those countries where they are carried on extensively and to the best advantage, the women of the whole country around are employed as much as possible. The managers of the American manufactory in this city, being desirous to extend the circle of this part of the business wish to employ every good spinner that can apply, however remote from the factory, as many women in the country may supply themselves with the materials there and may have leisure to spin considerable quantities, they are hereby informed that ready money will be given at the factory up Market Street, for any parcel, wither great or small, of hemp, flax or woolen yarn.*

The managers return their thanks to all those industrious women who are now employed in spinning for the factory; the skill and diligence of many entitles them to the public acknowledgment. We hope as you have begun, so you will go on, and never be weary in well doing." ~ **The Pennsylvania Packet, Philadelphia**

1776

118.   This was a poem that Phillis Wheatley wrote for George Washington. It was printed in many of the newspapers of the day. The poem is prefaced with a short note from Phillis in her own words.

March 30, 1776 – **Phillis Wheatley.** *"Monsieur's Dixon and Hunter, pray insert the enclosed letter and verses, written by the famous Phillis Wheatley, the African poetess, in your next gazette.*

Sir, I have taken the freedom to address your Excellency in the enclosed poem, and entreat your acceptance, though I am not insensible of its inaccuracies. You're being appointed by the Grand Continental Congress to be Generalissimo of the armies of North America, together with the same of your virtues, excite sensations not easy to suppress. Your generosity, therefore, I presume, will pardon the attempt. Wishing you Excellency all possible success in the great cause you are so generously engaged in, I am your Exellency's most obedient humble servant, Phillis Wheatley."

To his Excellency General Washington

Celestial choir! Enthron'd in realms of light,
Columbia's scenes of glorious toils I write.
While freedom's cause her anxious breast alarms
She flashes dreadful in refulgent arms.
See mother earth her offspring's fate bemoan,
And nations gaze at scenes before unknown!
See the bright beams of heaven's revolving light
Involv'd in sorrows and the veil of night!
The goddess comes, she moves divinely fair,
Olive and laurel bind her golden hair:
Wherever shines this native of the skies
Unnumber'd charms and recent graces rise.
Muse! Bow propitious, while my pen relates
How pour her armies through a thousand gates:
As when Eolus heaven's fair face deforms,
Enwrap'd in tempest, and a night of storms;
Astonishe'd ocean feels the wild uproar,

The refluent surges beat the sounding shore;
Or thick as leaves in autumn's golden reign,
Such, and so many, moves the warrior train.
In bright array they seek the work of war,
Where high unfurl'd the ensign waves in air.
Shall I to Washington their praise recite?
Enough thou know'st them in the fields of fight.
Thee, first in place and honors, we demand
The grace and glory of thy martial band.
Fam'd for thy valour, for thy virtues more,
Hear every tongue thy guardian aid implore!
One century fearce perform'd its destin'd round,
When Gallic powers Columbia's fury found;
And so may you, whoever dares disgrace
The land of freedom's heaven-defended race!
Fix'd are the eyes of nations on the scales,
For in their hopes Columbia's arm prevails.
Anon Britannia droops the pensive head,
While round increase the rising hills of dead.
Ah! Cruel blindness to Columbia's state!
Lament thy thirst of boundless power too late.
Proceed, great chief, with virtue on thy side,
Thy every action let the goddess guide.
A crown, a mansion, and a throne that shine,
With gold unfading, Washington! Be thine." ~ **The Virginia Gazette, Williamsburg, VA**

119.   Mother of Thomas Jefferson dies **March 31, 1776** – Jane Randolph Jefferson, mother of US president Thomas Jefferson (b. 1720-d.1776)

120.   Abigail Adams wrote these words to her husband, John Adams, on March 31, 1776. - **Abigail Adams**. *"I long to hear that you have declared an independency. And, by the way, in the new code of laws which I suppose it will be necessary for you to make, I desire you would remember the ladies and be more generous and favorable to them than your ancestors. Do not put such unlimited power into the hands of the husbands. Remember, all men would be tyrants if they could. If*

particular care and attention is not paid to the ladies, we are determined to foment a rebellion, and will not hold ourselves bound by any laws in which we have no voice or representation." [LOC.gov]

121.   1776 – *"Mrs. Sarah Goddard, was also a printer at Newport. She was born in Rhode Island, and widow of Giles Goddard, a printer of New London. She received a good education and well acquainted with many branches of literature. She had the management of a newspaper and conducted it with much ability for two years when John Carter associated with her under the firm of Sarah Goddard & Co."* ~ **The Brooklyn Daily Eagle, Brooklyn, New York**

For context of where we are in history: The Declaration of Independence is signed on August 2, 1776. Our first president, George Washington will not elected president until the year 1789.

When The Declaration of Independence is signed there are 13 states in the Union:

New Hampshire, Massachusetts, Connecticut, Rhode Island, New York, New Jersey, Pennsylvania, Delaware, Maryland, Virginia, North Carolina, South Carolina and Georgia which were originally founded in 1607. Often referred to, at the time, as the British Colonies or, the American Colonies. The men forming the colonies strongest belief was "no taxation without representation". A justification the women would use not only in their fight for the right to vote, but for other rights as well.

New Jersey drafts its first constitution in 1776. The first to expand the right to vote specifically to unwed female landholders and black land owners.

The <u>New Jersey</u> constitution of 1776 enfranchised (allowed them to vote) all adult inhabitants who owned a specified amount of property. Laws enacted in 1790 and 1797 referred to voters as "he or she", and women regularly voted. A law passed in 1807, however, excluded women from voting in that state.

"IV. That all inhabitants of this Colony, of full age, who are worth fifty pounds proclamation money, clear estate in the same, and have resided within the county in which they claim a vote for twelve months immediately preceding the election, shall be entitled to vote for Representatives in Council and Assembly; and also for all other public officers, that shall be elected by the people of the county at large." <u>New Jersey</u> 1776"

This measure was replaced in 1844 by an all white male administration in New Jersey. This new state constitution specifically denied not only women the right to vote, but also African-Americans.

Mary Philbrook, the first female attorney in the state of New Jersey challenged this law in 1912, taking it all the way to the New Jersey Supreme Court arguing that women should have the right to vote. 'Carpenter v Cornish' argue that the Constitution of 1776 gave all inhabitants the vote; which, in her argument included women. The New Jersey Supreme Court upheld the 1844 measure citing that women were not given the right to vote in the 1776 Constitution.

amrevmuseum.org/virtualexhibits/when-women-lost-the-vote-a-revolutionary-

story/pages/defeating-woman-suffrage-in-new-jersey

122.   *August 30, 1776 – "There never was an instance of fortunes being made by foreigners more quietly and in general more*

unsuspected, than by the Queen's German women. Mrs. Schwellenbergen has above 100,000L in our funds, with near as much more in the banks of Hambro and Amsterdam. Mrs. Hagerdorn has 30,000L in the funds, and has laid out 13,000L in the purchase of an estate in Mecklenburgh and Mrs. Guydiakens has also made a considerable fortune. The salaries of their offices are utterly incompetent to such profits, but they have the means without the assistance of their royal mistress, to stock job, and that would explain almost any fortune." ~ Harrison's Derby Journal, Derbyshire, England

123.   *September 5, 1776 – "(Philadelphia) Since the departure of the able bodied men from the forks of Brandywine, in Chester County, on the service of their country, the patriotic young women to prevent the evil that would follow the neglect of putting in the fall crop in season, have joined the ploughs, and are preparing the sallows for the feed and should their fathers, brothers and lovers be detained abroad in defense of the liberties of these states they are determined to put in the crop themselves. A very laudable example and highly worthy of imitation."* ~ The Maryland Gazette, Annapolis, MD

1777

South Carolina General Gazette, Jan 16, 1777 (this enterprising young woman had her ad on the front page of the South Carolina General Gazette!)

January 16, 1777 *- "Elisabeth Martha Wells, opposite Dr. Ramsay's in Broad Street, begs leave to acquaint the publick, that she carries on the *Mantua Making Business in all its branches and will make it her study to give satisfaction to those who are pleased to employ her."* ~ South Carolina General Gazette

**Muntua Making, as I understand it, is a unique type of sewing.*

124.   In 1777 an American woman, dressed as a man, killed seven British troops during the American Revolutionary War. It was reported in the Public Advertiser, a newspaper in London: [April 8, 1777] – *"An American woman, in the habit of a man, killed seven of our troops in the late skirmishes in the Jerseys. Her sex was not discovered till she was shot by an English Sargent, after her regiment, to their great surprise, discovered the supposed provincial solder to be a woman. A soldier lately arrived from New York was wounded in the leg by the above heroine, after which it was obliged to be cut off."* ~ The Public Advertiser, London, England

125. I found the following news article dated June 1777 in the Osage County Chronicle, Kansas, describing the meeting between Betsy Ross, George Washington and the committee that had been formed to decide the design of a flag for our nation.

    June 1777 – "At the residence of Mrs. Betsy Ross, a relative of Colonel George Ross, in Arch Street, between Second and Third, where General Washington and the committee completed the design for a suitable flag for the nation employed Mrs. Ross to execute the work. The design was for a flag of thirteen red and white stripes, alternate, with a union, blue in the field, spangled with thirteen six pointed stars. Mrs. Ross expressed her willingness to make the flag but suggested that the stars would be more symmetrical and pleasing to the eye if made with five points and she showed them how such a star could be made; by folding a sheet of paper and producing the pattern by a single cut. Her plan was approved and she at once proceeded to make the flag which was finished the next day. Mrs. Ross was given the position of manufacturer of flags and uniforms for the government." ~ The Osage County Chronicle, Burlingame, Kansas

The following is the case of two men, who have taken a bet on the gender of a person, male or female, all the way to the courts!

126.   *July 4, 1777 – "THE SEX OF D'EON DETERMINED. On Tuesday morning came on a cause to be tried in the court of King's Bench at Guildhall before Lord Mansfield and a special jury. The final*

decision of which is of the utmost importance to every person concerned in the policies opened on the sex of the Chevalier D'Eon.

The action was brought by Mr. Hayes, a surgeon, in Leicester-Fields, against one Jacques, a broker and underwriter, for the recovery of fifteen guineas for which he stood engaged to return one hundred guineas whenever it should be proved, that the Chevalier D'Eon was actually a woman.

Mr. Buller opened the cause, as counsel for Mr. Hayes. He stated the fairness of the transaction and justifiable nature of the demand, as Mr. Hayes, the plaintiff, though himself now to be in possession of that proof, which would determine the sex of the Chevalier D'Eon, and forever render the case indisputable.

In proof of the fact, Mr. Le G., a surgeon, was the first witness called. He gave his testimony to the following effect:

'That he had been acquainted with the Chevalier D'Eon, from the time when the Duc de Nivernois resided in England, in quality of Ambassador from the Court of France. That to his certain knowledge, the person called the Chevalier D'Eon was a woman.'

Being closely interrogated by the counsel for the defendant, as to the mode of his acquiring such a degree of certainty relative to the sex of the party, Mr. Le G. gave this satisfactory account of the matter:

'That about five years ago he was called in by the Chevalier D'Eon, to lend his professional aid for her assistance. The D'Eon unfortunately for herself, as well as her sex labored at that time under a disorder which rendered an examination of the afflicted part absolutely necessary. That this examination led, of course, to that discover of the sex, of which Mr. Le G. was now enabled to give such satisfactory testimony.'

The second witness called on the part of the plaintiff was Mr. de M. He swore: 'that so long ago as the 3rd of July 1774 the Chevalier D'Eon made a free disclosure of her sex to the witness. That she had even proceeded so far as to display her bosom on the occasion. That in consequence of this disclosure of sex, she, had exhibited the contents of her female wardrobe, which consisted of sacques, petticoats, and other habiliments, calculated for feminine use. That on the said third day of July the witness paid a morning visit to D'Eon and finding her in bed accosted her in a style of gallantry respecting her sex. That so far from being offended with this freedom, the said Chevalier desired the witness to approach nearer to her bed, and then permitted him to have manual proof of her being in truth a very woman.'

The counsel for the defendant endeavored to give a turn of humor to his testimony, by ascribing the indecent liberties allowed by mademoiselle D'Eon to French levity. The fact, however, was incontrovertibly established.

The testimony of Mr. de M. went also to prove other facts of a political nature, which had a collateral respect unto the sex of D'Eon. A negotiation for the return of this lady to France had been entrusted to the conduct of De M. She was to have made a restitution of certain papers to Mr. B., who acted as an agent from the court of France on the occasion. An annuity of five hundred pounds had been agreed on besides sundry sums of money which were paid into the hands of D'Eon, as valuable considerations for the restitution. During the whole of these negotiations D'Eon had been treated as a woman by the parties, and had allowed herself to be recognized as such in the writings respecting the transaction.

The third witness called in proof of the sex of the Chevalier, was Doctor De M., a French physician. Being sworn he gave the following testimony:

'That, from his own knowledge he was certain that the Chevalier was a woman. That he had attended her, in quality of a physician, at a certain period when disorders incident to the softer sex required his professional skill. That he had had every sensible proof of her sex, which sight and touch could convey.'

The evidence and the pleadings of counsel on the part of the plaintiff having been gone through Mr. Mansfield, in behalf of the defendant endeavored to prove:

That the contract should be nullified as Mr. Hays was possessed of the proof of the sex of the person at the time he proposed to Mr. Jacques to underwrite the policies.

As a decisive reply to this assertion, the answer of Mr. Hayes to a Bill in Chancery filed against him by Jacques, was read. In that answer Mr. Hayes had declared on oath:

That when he paid the premiums on the sex of D'Eon he had no other reason to believe her to be a woman than the common rumor of persons on whose testimony he thought he could confide.

That T. and T., esquire, had originally apprized him of the sex of D'Eon but he had not given any certain proof of the fact.

That Mr. A., now Sir Robert A., Mr. C., now Sir John C., and Mr. S., had accompanied the Chevalier into the country. During her continuance with them they had had an effort to prevail on her to disclose her sex. She had rejected the proposal.

That in consequence of the failure of this effort he, Mr. Hayes, entertained a doubt respecting the sex of the Chevalier, and not thinking the premiums which he had ventured on the policies to be secure he had sold a moiety of them to Baron N., the S. Envoy.

These assertions clearly refuted the charge of fraudulency urged against Mr. Hayes, by the counsel for the defendant.

Mr. Wallace then made a final reply on the part of the plaintiff. He contended that the defendant had exclaimed against the indecency of bringing such a cause before a court of judicature. This was only a fallacious mode of evading the payment of a just demand. Why not bring the matter to an issue? The decision was of consequence. The proofs of the fact were clear. Not a single evidence had contested fact. What had the defendant to alleged?

That the plaintiff had wagered a sum, which, from his superior knowledge of the case he was sure to win! Every man who laid a wager considered himself likely to be the winner. But, if the objection carried any weight, it would operate with a treble force against the defendant. Jacques had laid seven to one that D'Eon was a man. He that lays the odds, must think himself better secure in his wager, than the man who accepts them.

Lord Mansfield then charged the jury in the following words:

Gentlemen of the jury, this is a gambling debt. I wish it were possible to abolish all debts of the kind. I should be glad if your verdict could so operate as that neither party might be the winner. As one of them must lose, you have only to consider which of them ought to win.

With respect to the contract on which the action is founded, there is not anything illegal in it. It is binding on both parties. The discovery of the sex of a certain person is to give it operation. Each party thought himself certain of the fact. There was every external proof that the defendant was right in his conjecture. D'Eon dressed as a man. She would have fought duels. She was a Captain of Dragoons. Resided here as ambassador. To all outward appearance, therefore, the defendant had the best of the wager. On the part of the plaintiff there was a considerable difficulty. Suppose him to have been right, yet the proof of the fact was not easy. It was not in the power of any person to compel D'Eon to disclose her sex. Was it known, the proof still rested on the plaintiff. He had so far the disadvantageous side of the question.

It hath been thrown out that he was sure of the fact at the time he laid the wager. The contrary hath appeared. He had not proofs in his power at the time the contract was entered into. The court of France was not apprised of the fact. That court considered D'Eon as a man. There were reasons afterwards to believe the contrary. When those reasons were made known, that court directed the matter to be thoroughly investigated. Still it might have been difficulty to prove the sex, if the private quarrels of the party had not furnished such collateral evidence as put the question out of doubt.

On the part of the defendant there appears to have been a backwardness to bring the cause into court. The indecency was urged. There is nothing indecent in the business. The witnesses have sworn to the fact on their own knowledge. They are either perjured or you must credit their testimonies.

As to the certainty of either of the parties, it hath been well observed that they both conceived themselves certain of winning. This is the case in all wagers. I remember a dispute which once happened between two persons relative to the dimensions of a statue of the Venus de Medici. A wager was proposed by one of the parties. The other replied I will not lay anything. It would be unfair, for I have measured the statue. The other answered, why you think I would be such a fool as to propose a bet unless I had measured it also. The wager was laid.

You will consider all circumstances. If you think that the bet is fairly won, you will decide in favor of the plaintiff.

The jury, without hesitation gave a verdict for the plaintiff, seven hundred pounds and forty shillings.

Lord Mansfield behaved to a charm. He supported the dignity of justice and the impartiality of truth. He detected the imposture of the sex, without exposing the iniquity of the pretension. He ridiculed the woman in masquerade, without questioning the courage of the Captain of Dragoons.

Besides the seven hundred pounds given by verdict to Mr. Hayes, he will recover 3000 pounds on other policies.

The sex of Mademoiselle D'Eon being legally substantiated in a court of judicature, the numerous tribe of policyholders will now be

*astonished that the secret should have been so long and so well
observed.*

*Immense sums in policies were depending on the suit which was
on Tuesday determined against the manhood of Mademoiselle
D'Eon."* ~ The Derby Mercury, England

127.　　July 14, 1777 – **Phillis Wheatley wrote the following Letter to
the Editor in July of 1777.**

"To the Printer of the Public Advertiser.

*One of your correspondents, who, some weeks since, drew his grey
goose quill against Miss Hannah Moore, seems to plume himself as if
he had fairly laid her on her back. That lady, sir, is not on the spot to
answer for herself, and to attack a lady behind her back is surely no
proof of your correspondents understanding; for I will venture to
affirm that if she thought it worth her while to receive this doughty
enemy face to face she would soon give him such a brush as would
make him drop his ears, and retreat from the charge.*

*But as she is not at present in town I am ready to have a touch
with this same white faced enemy of modern poetesses; and
though I cannot boast of such capacity as Miss More, I think I can
knock him down in his own way. It will I assure you, be a black
affair for him if, to use a sea phrase, he comes under my Lee. For I
will have no mercy on a man who stands up against me on that
score. As I know nothing of your correspondent, I desire that you
will convey to him this fair challenge; and let him produce his
charge as soon as he pleases, and he may find that I will not shrink
back in the combat.*

*He holds up his crest, no doubt, with confidence, as he has
hitherto met with no rub for his impudence in turning up the frail
part of us female poets; but I would have him draw back in time
and not plunge too deep into a subject whose bottom his short line
of understanding can never fathom. I have in my time knocked off
many a better pen than his, and therefore, sir, if he is a friend of
yours you had better advise him to turn the muzzle of his
blunderbuss to some other quarter. This doughty warrior of yours
may make some figure upon opponents of no experience, but I
know too much of mankind, and have so often taken the measure
of their understanding, that I am not afraid to grapple with any
literary male in the kingdom. Tho' I cannot boast of such extensive
parts as the great female historian, or what is more the lady your*

correspondent attacks at unawares, I persuade myself, narrow as I confide my capacity that I am a match for the stiffest pedant in the republic of letters.

If your correspondent, therefore, means to try his strength, I hope this will be considered by him as a fair warning to come as well provided as he can to the field, that he may have it in his power, by making a good stand, to diminish the disgrace of his defeat. Signed, Phillis Wheatley." ~ **The Public Advertiser, London, England**

wikipedia.org/wiki/Hannah_More

phillis-wheatley.org/later-life-death/

128.

Lydia Darragh, an assumed spy in Philadelphia lived across the street from General Howe during the war, in 1777. General William Howe was the General of the British land forces. In other words, the enemy during the American Revolutionary War. She died in 1789 but by the 1800s newspapers were printing 'rumors' about her involvement in spying on General Howe for George Washington and the success of the Continental Army. I found the following news story from July 1777 of an unnamed female spy that I wonder could it be the Lydia Darragh named in the 1800s.. (Tories were American Colonist who supported the British side during the American Revolutionary War.)

July 18, 1777 – A Female Spy. *"A spy is brought in here with letters of importance to General Howe and it is said to another person whom one would not suspect. The contents have not transpired. The other day a pretty strong detachment went from this place to Cherry Valley to keep the Tories in awe. It is currently reported that*

Ticonderoga will soon be visited. Many people are in confinement here.

A woman who left New York about ten days ago says that 300 of the Tories who lately went thither but attempting to get off again were in one night impressed and conveyed on board the shipping in order as was thought to be transported to some of the British Garrisons abroad.

We hear that in the course of last week 60 of the enemy, in Jersey were taken prisoners." ~ **Virginia Gazette, Williamsburg, VA**

129.   July 23, 1777 – In answer to the July, 1777 Letter to the Editor from **Phillis Wheatley.** *"To the printer of the Public Advertiser. Sir, I am sorry to find from Phillis Wheatley's Letter in your paper of the 14th that she has taken in dudgeon some late strictures of mine on certain modern poetesses. It is true, she was likewise mentioned on that occasion, but in a manner, I hope, that could give her no just offense and to convince her that I meant no injury.*

I send the following Palinode, which, if you think fit to publish it, may be sufficient to pacify her resentment. I might have justified myself in prose, but I preferred the language of Parnassus, as being more suitable to the dignity of the object.

Palinode to Phillis Wheatley:

'Tis not a set of features or complexion, the tincture of a skin that I admire ~ Addison.

Poetic Queen of parched whidaw!
With sable beauties, void of flaw,
Obscurely like the night,
Steal softly to my throbbing breast,
Where cupid dwells, the little guest,
Who hates the garish light.

Like Phoebe in eclipse you move,
A dark portent of fatal love
To those who fight in vain,
Unbend on me, with gentle smile,
Your disky features for awhile.
Deceive or heal my pain.

Let others sigh for brighter charms,
For rosy necks and round white arms,
And call all beauty fair
My soul is fixed on nymphs, who lave
Their woolly locks in niger's wave
And black is all my care.

Why do these eyes in passion roll?
Thou Ebon tyrant of my soul!
Expel this causeless spite!
I never meant to Phillis harm,
Nor winged one shaft at sooty charm.
My rage was aimed at white.

Should even my dusky beauty choose
To shield each daughter of the muse
Who deals in classic lore.
For her their nonsense I'll forgive,
In Christian patience with them live,
Nay, I'll do something more!" ~ **The Public Advertiser London, England**

130.
August 8, 1777 – *"Last Tuesday about 11 o'clock in the forenoon, arrived here, from the seat of Burwell Bassett, Esquire's, in New Kent,* **Lady Washington***, the amiable consort of his Excellency General Washington. Upon her arrival she was saluted with the fire of cannon and small arms, and was safely conducted to Mrs. Dawson's in this city, and intends setting out for the northward in a few days." At a meeting of the Common Hall of this city, on Friday to take into their consideration the arrival of General Washington's Lady they came to the following resolutions:*
That a golden emblematical medal be prepared to be presented to the General's Lady as the most suitable method of carrying that design into execution and that the mayor be desired to form the device and agree with some proper persons to execute the same." ~ **Virginia Gazette, Williamsburg, VA**

131.

In August of 1777 seven black women and a child were discovered on a deserted island. Here is their story as reported in the newspapers at that time:

August 23, 1777 – Amsterdam: *"A letter from Port Louis, in the Isle of France, elucidates the conjectures and doubts that had arisen concerning the unfortunate shipwrecked people who were lately seen upon a sandy island, and were supposed to be the remainder of the crew of the Aurora Frigate which sailed from England some years ago with the East India supervisors on board. It is now certain that they are the surviving part of the crew of an Asiatic ship, wrecked on that bank in 1761, being eight in number, one of whom is a European. The letter gives the following account of that interesting matter:*

The Dauphine, a King's Cutter, commanded by the Chevalier Lanugny Tromelin, a Lieutenaut, who left this port the 25th last November, being sent to reconnoiter the Sable Island, and to take off some blacks, who had been formerly perceived there by many ships is returned and brings the following account:

*The 28th of November, at sunset, they discovered the island and the 29th the weather being very fine and almost a calm, Mr. Le Sage, an officer of the cutter, was dispatched with a boat and a canoe to the west of the island, from whence he brought back **seven black women** and a Negro child eight months old. They were the only people existing on the island. Those wretched creatures, being interrogated as to their unhappy situation, said, that they had been on that island ever since the loss of the Indiaman called L'Utile, wrecked there the 3rd of July 1761. That the most part of the crew left them, taking to their boat leaving about eighty black men and women, eighteen of whom, sometime after, embarked on a sort of raft, made with planks fastened on masts, which they got from the wreck, and had never come back; that, within these 12 years their number had been reduced to thirteen the rest having died through fatigue and want.*

These women say that during the space of 15 years which they have been there, they have only seen five ships, who, upon signals made to them all attempted to land, but, from the great danger attending such attempts, were obliged to desist; that, some time ago, a ship called La Sauterelle, sent a boat on shore and gave them some assistance but the weather being boisterous next day prevented the boat coming again to take them off. That one of the sailors belonging to the boat taking a fancy to one of them staid on the island, intending to go on board his ship next day when the boat came back but being as well as they, disappointed, was obliged to take up his residence among them. About three months ago he embarked on another raft, with three black men, and three women, in hopes of reaching the island of Madagascar.

The manner in which these unfortunate people lived, after their shipwreck, on that desert island as well as can be collected from those brought here was as follows:

They built, from the wreck of the ship, a sort of a cabin on the most elevated part of the island and covered it with the shells of turtles which they caught in great abundance and on which they chiefly subsisted. They likewise by way of change of diet caught some fish and a few birds with their eggs. They dug a hole in the sand, which supplied them with a brackish kind of water being their only drink. The feathers of the birds which they caught curiously worked together was their coverage.

The island is a quarter of a league in length and three hundred perches in breadth. Its highest part is about fifteen feet. The violence of the sea has thrown up on its banks all around a quantity of coral and sand by which means the centre of the island is much lower than the sides. There is neither grass, tree nor shrub, grows on it nor any kind of vegetable except a kind of potato, or during which grows among the sand. The whole island is surrounded with breakers, which extend upwards of a hundred and fifty fathoms to the south and are very near the shore on the north side. These people say that in bad weather which happens very often the wind almost covered their hut with sand and that they were in constant fear of being swallowed by the sea." **~Jackson's Oxford Journal, Oxfordshire, England**

132.　*November 27, 1777 –* A Woman Posing as a Soldier. *"The following extraordinary circumstance happened on Monday evening last. Two soldiers of the first regiment of foot guards enlisted a recruit in Westminster. They took him to the orderly room at the House Guards, and had him measured but the approving officer not being present, he could not then be allowed, however they took him to the hospital to have him examined by the surgeon. This the recruit absolutely refused to comply with, nor could persuade. Suspecting something extraordinary to be the matter they by force proceeded to an examination and to their no small mortification and surprise, found they had inspected a woman. They took her before a justice and had her committed as an imposter."* ~ The Newport Gazette, Newport, RI

In Connecticut, Mrs. Watson, the widow of Ebenezar Watson, who died in 1777, continued one of the publishers of the Courant at Hartford for two years, when a gentlemen of "steady habits" took her as a sleeping partner. The Courant is still published.

Brooklyn Daily Eagle, Brooklyn, NY

1778

133.   *August 8, 1778* – Rest In Peace. *"Mrs. Ross (formerly Fanny Murray) though from her early starting in public life, known for a succession of years to all ranks of people, has only the age of 49 marked on her coffin."* ~ Pennsylvania Packet

Mrs. Rofs (formerly Fanny Murray) though from her early ftarting in public life, known for a fucceffion of years to all ranks of people, has only the age of 49 marked on her coffin.

Pennsylvania Packet, Aug 8, 1778

Fanny Murray was born in 1729 in Bath, England. It is thought that the scandalous 'Essay on Woman' written in 1763 by John Wilkes was dedicated to Fanny Murray, aka Fanny Rudman and sometimes known as Fanny Ross.

Fanny was a known prostitute who developed a level of celebrity about herself and became a fashion leader in her community.

134.   *April 10, 1778 – "BROAD CREEK ON NEUSE RIVER. On Saturday night, broke into the house of the subscriber at the head of Green's Creek, where I had some small property under the care of Ann Driggus, a free negro woman, two men in disguise, who with marks on their faces and clubs in their hands beat and wounded her terribly and carried away four of her children, three girls and a boy, the biggest of the said girls got off in the dark and made her escape, one of the girl's name is Becca, and the other Charita, the boy is named Shadrock; she says the men were William Munday and Charles Towzer, a sailor lately from Newbern, these men were on board of a boat belonging to Kelly Cason, and was with him in the boat about the middle of the day. Fifty dollars reward will be given to any person who will stop the children and apprehend the robbers so that they may be brought to justice. John Caruthers."* ~ The North Carolina Weekly Gazette, New Bern, April 10, 1778

135.   July 3, 1778 – Died. Anna Maria Mozart, mother of Wolfgang Amadeus Mozart and Maria Anna Mozart has died. She was 57 years old. Her daughter Maria Anna was also a celebrated musician. She performed with Wolfgang in concert and is considered to be quite talented. Anna Maria chaperoned her two children, Wolfgang and Maria Anna on tour when her children, both under the age of 13, were being touted as prodigies.

I found this newspaper ad for one of their joint concerts from February 11, 1765 in the Public Advertiser, London, England:

For the Benefit of Mifs MOZART of Twelve, and Mafter MOZART of Eight Years of Age : Prodigies of Nature. LITTLE Theatre in the Hay-market, Friday, Feb. 15, will be a Concert of Vocal and Inftrumental MUSIC. Tickets, at Half a Guinea each, to be had of Mr. Mozart, at Mr. Williamfon's in Thrift-ftreet, S ho

wikipedia.org/wiki/Anna_Maria_Mozart

1779

136.   On April 8, 1779 Peggy Shippen married Benedict Arnold, his second wife. Peggy was reportedly the highest paid spy in the American Revolution. She and Benedict had seven children

137.   *"**Female Heroism Rewarded.** [Journals of Congress July 6, 1779] Resolved, that **Margaret Corbin**, who was wounded and disabled in the attack on Fort Washington, whilst she heroically filled the post of her husband, who was killed by her side, serving a piece of artillery, do receive, during her natural life, or the continuance of the said disability, the one half of the monthly pay drawn by a soldier in the service of these States; and that she now receive, out of the public stores, one complete suit of clothes or the value thereof in money."* ~ Aurora General Advertiser, Philadelphia, PA

138.

PHILADELPHIA.

In GENERAL ASSEMBLY, November 16, 1779.
The Bill intitled " A Supplement to the Act for the relief of the Poor," was read a second time, and being debated by paragraphs, was ordered to be tranfcribed for a third reading and publifhed for confideration.
Extract from the Minutes,
THOMAS PAINE,
Clerk of the General Affembly.

"and be it further enacted that from and after the publication of this Act, the widows of such commissioned military officers as have fallen in battle or died in actual service or captivity, and whose husbands, if they had lived would have been entitled to such half pay, and those who may hereafter become the widows, of officers to falling in battle, or dying in actual service or captivity, during the continuance of the present war, shall be entitled to the half of the pay which their husbands, were respectively entitled to whilst in said service during their widowhood and no longer.

And be it further enacted that on the petition of any of said widows, to the orphans court, in any county in this state, the said court shall in a summery way enquire into the claim of such widow to the half pay allowed by this Act and the said court on receiving satisfactory proof of the marriage and that the husband of the said widow would, if he had lived, have been entitled to half pay under this Act, which proof shall be by a certificate under the hand and seal of the Colonel or other commanding officer of the regiment, battalion or company to which the deceased last belongs setting forth the commission which he last held to include the time and place of his death. Such certificate to be attested under the hands of two witnesses or in the case of the widow of such commanding officer from the officer next in command.

It is further enacted that the Orphans Court shall once in three months of every year examine the record of such annuities and send an authentic list of the said widows and sums of which they are entitled to the county treasurer." ~Pennsylvania Packet, Philadelphia, Nov 25, 1779

1780

MUSINGS

Cordova in the Tucuman, June 1, 1779. In the Village of Altagratia there lives a Negro Woman, who, according to the moſt authentic information and teſtimonies taken judicially, muſt be about 175 years old : She is extremely thin, very much wrinkled, and bent double, but ſhe can ſee at a few paces diſtant, and ſpins ; but what is moſt extraordinary, though ſhe cannot ſtand for any ſpace of time, ſhe ſtill carries on the buſineſs of a midwife with dexterity. She had five children by her huſband, one Michael, a Negro ; and ſhe thinks her grandchildren have grand-children of their own. Old people ſeem to be no rarity in that country, as there are ſeveral Negroes upwards of 100 years old, and one woman of 110, who retains her memory perfectly, and declares that the old woman in queſtion was arrived at woman's eſtate when ſhe firſt had the uſe of her reaſon.

Pennsylvania Packet, Philadelphia, PA, May 9, 1780

139.Caroline Herschel, (B:1750-D:1848), was the first woman to discover a comet and the first woman to have her work published by the Royal Society. She is the first British woman to be paid for her scientific work.

140.   *October 27, 1780 – "On Friday the 17th past the Caesarian operation was performed at the infirmary in Leicester. The unfortunate woman died in consequence of the operation but the boy who was then taken from his mothers side is still alive."* ~ The Derby Mercury, England

1781

141.   *February 17, 1781 –* In 1781 Thomas Jefferson was the Governor of Virginia. In January and February there was a battle with the Cherokees. Thomas Jefferson shared a letter from Colonel Campbell with the newspapers of the day. *"[...] the **famous Indian woman Nancy Ward** (Nanyehi) came to camp. She gave us various intelligence and made an overture in behalf of some of the Chiefs for peace to which I then evaded giving an explicit answer as I wished first to visit the vindictive part of the nation, mostly settled at Hiwaffee and Chiftowee and to distress the whole as much as possible by destroying their habitations and provisions. [...] By the end of the battle we had killed 29 men and took 17 prisoners, mostly women and children. Besides these we brought in the family of Nancy Ward whom for their good offices we do not consider as prisoners."* ~ The Pennsylvania Packet, Philadelphia, Mar 13, 1781

Nancy Ward: aka Nanyehi, was born circa 1738 and was the leader of the Cherokee. She was known as one who advocated for peace. Nanyehi reportedly went into battle alongside her husband, Tsula aka Kingfisher. For her bravery the Cherokee made her the only woman with the privilege of voting on the Cherokee General Council. By July of 1781 Nanyehi was able to negotiate a peace treaty with the Americans

142. In August of 1781 a black slave woman named Mum Bett, sometimes written as Mumbet filed suit against the state of Massachusetts that she should be a free woman. She was the first enslaved black person to file

such a suit and win. On August 22, 1781 a jury in Massachusetts concluded that she should be free. A quote from Mum Bet, aka Elizabeth Freeman, the name she used after gaining her freedom, has always moved me:

"Any time, while I was a slave, if one minute's freedom had been offered to me, and I had been told I must die at the end of that minute, I would have taken it. Just to stand one minute on God's earth a free woman. Yes, I would. ~ Elizabeth Freeman"

The case, known as Brom and Bett v Ashley, 1781 was used in later cases as precedent.

She was born into slavery in the year 1744 in New York. Ashley was the name of the woman who "owned" her. The case was heard in Barrington, Massachusetts. After the ruling she went to work for the attorney who had taken her case; for wages. She passed away in 1829 and is buried in the attorney's family plot.

143. Martha Washington's only remaining child, her son John, dies on **November 5, 1781** at age 26. He had developed typhus while serving in the American Revolutionary War. Martha and George did not have any children of their own. Upon the death of her son John, who had four children with his wife Eleanor, George and Martha took in the two youngest grandchildren while the two older children stayed to be raised by their mother. George and Martha were in the White House from 1789-1797.

1782

144. Deborah Sampson (B:1760-D:1827) joined the American Revolutionary War, as a soldier, dressed as a man under the name Robert Shirtliff. Her military record shows she served for a period of 17 months. She was wounded in 1782 and honorably discharged in 1783. An official record of her military service appears in the 'Massachusetts Soldiers and Sailors of the walRevolutionary War, Volume 14, page 164'.

Ms. Sampson petitioned the Massachusetts State Legislature for back pay for her service to the army, withheld only because she was a woman. She was, in fact, awarded her rightful wages; her petition signed by then Governor John Hancock.

Sampson was awarded wages for her time served but not a military pension. Finally, in 1809, and after many petitions, and letters from friends like Paul Revere she was granted a military pension. This was the first time a woman had petitioned for a military pension. She would die of yellow fever at the age of 66 on April 29, 1827.

You can find a statue of Deborah Sampson in

Sharon, Massachusetts in front of the public

library.

LEGISLATURE OF MASSACHUSETTS.

JANUARY 17, 1792.

A very extraordinary circumstance arrested the attention of the House this afternoon. A petition was presented by a Mrs. Deborah Gannett, who served with reputation as a soldier, three years in the army of the United States, and received an honourable discharge therefrom. This extraordinary woman enlisted as a male, by the name of Robert Shurtliff, and as such, did her duty without a stain on her virtue or honour. She only prays, in her petition, for the payment of her arrears; but submits the circumstances of her services to the consideration of the Legislature: and from the feelings which appeared on the occasion, expressive of a desire to reward heroism like hers, there is no room to doubt that a compensation will be granted, adequate to her services, and honourable to the government.

Several members corroborated the facts, stated in the petition; which was committed to a respectable committee.

145. Before getting into this next article I want to address my suspicion that the article may be referring to Mrs. Benedict Arnold, aka: Peggy Shippen. In 1781 Peggy Shippen and her

husband Benedict Arnold sailed (fled) to England. The article refers to the woman only as Mrs. A- so we don't really know for sure for whom they speak. However, in doing my research on Mrs. Peggy Shippen Arnold I found out that she was in fact in England and Europe during the time frame in question. What is your conclusion?

July 18, 1782 –

Mrs. Benedict Arnold (aka Peggy Shippen) I Presume? *"The following intelligence, as we have it from the first authority, we can assure our readers may be depended on.*

About six weeks before Christmas last, a woman, who called herself the Honorable Mrs. A., was introduced to the then Premier at his house in Downing Street on the recommendation of an American refugee of very celebrated reputation, as a person of the most exquisite abilities at intrigue.

Our spies at the Court of Versailles had about that time become too notorious, or had been so idle as not to have informed government of many matters which were absolutely necessary to be known. Mrs. A, on the first interview with Lord N. discovered such an uncommon genius in the line of finesse, that she was afterwards introduced to other members of the cabinet and at last to the King himself. In about six weeks, after several audiences, it was found she could be made useful, and, upon her own offer, she was sent to Brussels, with proper appointments and a select company of chosen servants.

After a fortnights stay in that city, she removed to Paris, and under pretense that the Environs of that city agreed with her health, she took a house in Nouburg de Louis XVIth, and set up a plain equipage: She frequented all public places occasionally and was at the court on all public days. At last, she never missed of being at all the Queen's concerts, as well as those of the Princes of the Blood and had the address to get herself publicly presented as an American woman of fashion, perfectly unacquainted with the French tongue. She was constantly at Franklin's Levee, and at that of the Ministers of Louis the XVIth, as being a supposed stranger to the French language. It happened that she frequently came into the choicest secrets of the Court of Versailles, which she constantly dispatched with the utmost secrecy and haste to London, by way of Ostend. At last, from her very curious enquiries, though done with the utmost art, and appearance of innocence, she began to be suspected and one day in the middle of the last month, while she was at court, a messenger was sent to her house, who took possession. Luckily she had an item of it by a gentleman at Paris, who, though not on so hazardous a business, had employments at Paris. She accordingly disguised herself, and leaving her household, and all her valuables behind, came safe to Dunkirk, from whence she got a pass to Ostend, and on Sunday the 23rd of June arrived in London, having narrowly escaped a public execution as a female spy.

It was through this lady's intelligence, that such complete information was gained of the sailing of the fleets for the East Indies, whereby Admirals Barrington and Kemenfelt made such valuable captures and frustrated the designs of our enemies in that quarter. She is said also to have obtained a complete account of the manner in which the Siege of Gibraltar was to be carried on and also some American intelligence of the greatest importance." ~ **The Derby Mercury, Derbyshire, England,**

146. This is the history of women. This is a letter to the editor from a woman in the year 1782. : ***September 25, 1782** – "Letter to the Editor from a Suffering Mother. I read your paper as often as I can get it from a kind neighbor, for my circumstances will not allow me to be one of your subscribers, though I would if I could. Believing you a are a free printer, I beg of you will indulge me with printing what follows and correct my spelling, lest real distress should be turned into ridicule by those who are the cause of it.*

The contractors who have engaged to furnish the army with garments had doubtless good reasons to give the credit specified in their contracts or they would not have agreed with the financier. But, dear sir, the poor women who are employed in such work, cannot get their money. Is it the fault of the contractors; the under contactors or their understrappers? I know many women who were formerly in prosperity but are now reduced to take work for the support of their ruined families. Some of the women, necessitous as they are, take in work as clandestinely as if they were secreting stolen goods. I know other respectable but poor industrious women who always depended on their work for the maintenance of their children. All these made garments for the army expecting to be paid on the delivery of their work; but some of them after having waited several months are told by their employers 'I have not got the money and I don't know when I shall have it'. When this is made public, we may know who thus grindeth the faces of the poor. Our distresses don't deserve less attention from the humane public than the situation of the holders of loan office certificates who claim but the promised payment of interest and can wait for the reimbursement of their capital. Signed, a suffering mother." ~ The Freeman's Journal, Philadelphia, PA

147.   On September 6, 1782 Martha Wayles Jefferson dies. She was the first wife of future President Thomas Jefferson. She was the mother of Martha Jefferson Randolph, Mary Jefferson Eppes, Lucy Elizabeth Jefferson, Lucy Elizabeth Jefferson I, and Jane Jefferson. She was 34 years old at the time of her death.

1783

148.   Catharine Macaulay published 'The History of England from the Accession to the Revolution'. It took eight volumes to publish the entirety of her work. The books were published between the years of 1763 and 1783. This made Ms. Macaulay the first female historian and first Englishwoman known as a historian. Ms. Macaulay became well-known and celebrated for her work overnight. She remained quite popular in society until in 1778 when Catharine, at age 47, married William Graham who was just 21 years old. Considered a scandal she fell into obscurity. From 1784-1785 she visited the America's, staying at Mount Vernon with George Washington and his family. This was four years before Washington became the first president of the United States. She dies in 1791 at age 60.

149.   December 1783:

Laſt Thurſday died in this town, Lady Dinah, aged 90 years, an African queen of the Ebo nation, was kidnapped and brought to this town 56 years ago, the king, her huſband, being killed in an engagement with ſome other nation, and ſhe brought off, leaving two children behind her to lament the loſs of a father killed, and a mother ſold to an American captain; ſhe was afterwards purchaſed by captain Adino Bulfinch, and in that family brought up all their children and grand children, with whom ſhe lived as happy as her circumſtances would admit, being impaired in her ſenſes from the time of her being ſold; in her always appeared a majeſtic delicacy, but ſhe is now at reſt.

—Bluſh chriſtians who boaſt of liberty!

December 23, 1783 – **Lady Dinah, the African Queen.** *"Last Thursday died in this town, Lady Dinah, aged 90 years, an African Queen of the Ebo nation, was kidnapped and brought to this town 56 years ago, the king, her husband, being killed in an engagement with some other nation, and she brought off, leaving two children behind her to lament to the loss of a father killed and a mother sold to an American Captain. She was afterward purchased by Captain Adino Bulfinch and in that family brought up all their children and grandchildren with whom she lived as happy as her circumstances would admit. Being impaired in here senses from the time of her being sold in her always appeared a majestic delicacy but she is now at rest."* ~ The Pennsylvania Packet, Philadelphia

1784

150.   January 1784 - As you can see, many, many women were involved in the newspaper publishing business during the 1700s! This is the obituary of Mary Holt:

> Mrs. Mary Holt, widow of John Holt, and publisher of the " New York Journal," in 1783, was appointed printer to this state. The paper did powerful service during the Revolution.

Brooklyn Daily Eagle, Brooklyn, New York

151.   *February 19, 1784 –* London: *"On Monday night was committed to Lancaster castle for further examination a person genteelly dressed in men's cloaths. Who afterwards proved to be a woman. It since appears that she hath travelled in various characters, such as merchant, captain, supercargo officer in the army, midshipman, and others. She says her name is Peggy Buchanan. That she was born at Glasgow and hath travelled two years in men's apparel. She is five feet two inches high, appears 20 years of age, dark hazel eyes, pitted with the small pox and dark hair which hangs in ringlets on her shoulders and had on when apprehended a red coat with metal buttons, striped waistcoat, a round hat, drab colored breeches, and boots. She is strongly suspected of committing various frauds at London, Liverpool, Holiwell, Warrington and other places."* ~The Pennsylvania Packet, Philadelphia

152.   December 5, 1784 - OBITUARY *"Last Lord's day died, Phillis Peters, formerly Phillis Wheatly, known to the literary world by her celebrated miscellaneous poems."* ~ Pennsylvania Packet, Philadelphia

> BOSTON, December 8.
>
> Accounts from the country assure us, that the crops of the last season have been more propitious than for several prior autumns, which we hope will make cash plentier among the farmers, than by their complaints they seem to indicate.
>
> Last Lord's day died, Phillis Peters, formerly Phillis Wheatly, known to the literary world by her celebrated miscellaneous poems.

1785

MUSINGS

> B O S T O N, June 6.
> The increase of prostitution in this town, says a
> correspondent, is incredible, and unless stopped in
> embryo, will be attended with very pernicious con-
> sequences. The officers of the town, whose business
> it is to confine those of that sex in the work-house,
> are the very frequenters of their infernal habitations,
> and seem rather to encourage their diabolical pro-
> ceedings than put a stop to them.

Pennsylvania Packet, Philadelphia, Jun 22, 1785 [transcription] "The increase of prostitution in this town, says a correspondent, is incredible, and unless stopped in embryo will be attended with very pernicious consequences. The officers of the town, whose business it is to confine those of that sex in the work houses, are the very frequenters of their infernal habitations and seem rather to encourage their diabolical proceedings than put a stop to them."

153.   July 12, 1785 – New Manufactory Wage Difference. *"You will inform the committee whether 8 shillings is the price paid to the principal persons concerned in the manufactory and whether there are not others who receive much lower wages? I reckon 8 shillings to be the average price of labor that we pay to men in our manufacture.*
What is the price paid to women employed in the manufacture? About 5 shillings per week.
What is the average price paid to children employed in the manurfacture? 4 shillings per week." ~ The Belfast Mercury, Northern Ireland

1786

154. **Eva Ekeblad**, the first female member of the Royal Swedish Academy of Sciences has died.

June 30, 1786 – *"On the 15th died at Linkoping, in Sweden, in the 62nd year of her age, the Countess de Ekeblad, a lady distinguished for her literary acquirements. She was a member of the Swedish Academy of Sciences, an instance to be paralleled only by another in Spain."* ~

On the 15th died at Linkoping, in Sweden, in the 62d year of her age, the Countefs de Ekeblad, a Lady diftinguifhed for her literary acquirements. She was a Member of the Swedifh Academy of Sciences, an inftance to be paralleled only by another in Spain.

Public Advertiser, Greater London, England, **June 30, 1786**

155. A rare obituary in the newspapers of a black woman: RIP Ms. Davis

Yefterday evening, about fix o'clock, a free black woman, named LinJa Davis, who followed the trade of a baker, though in apparent good health, fuddenly dropt down dead, as fhe was putting a batch of bread into an oven.

American Daily Advertiser, Philadelphia, Aug 25, 1786

156. Woman Entrepreneur in 1786 Jamaica: *October 19, 1786 – Montego Bay, Jamaica: "We hear from Black River that on Saturday a most violent storm of thunder, lightning and rain attended with heavy squalls of wind happened at that place which did considerable damage both in the village and adjacent country. We are told in particular that though the lightning descended upon a large house at Black River kept as a tavern by a free Mulatto woman, which it tore almost to pieces in a very surprising manner, together with a billard room and table adjoining."* ~ Pennsylvania Packet, Philadelphia

1787

A brave woman named Fanny.

Three Pounds Reward.

RAN AWAY on the night of the 14th Instant—A NEGRO WOMAN, named FANNY: had on and took with her when she went away, a black peelong bonnet, two striped short gowns and two of calico, a striped linsey petticoat and one of cotton, two shifts, one of them fine linen, one pair of calfskin pumps. It is supposed she has other cloaths, and has endeavoured to make exchanges; was marked on the cheeks in Guinea, from whence she came when young; but the marks are not so visible since she has had the smallpox; one of her eyes opens a little wider than the other, and one of her knees bends inward more than the other; supposed to be rather better than five feet high. Whoever secures said negro woman so that the owner may have her again, shall have the above reward and reasonable charges paid, by

THOMAS JOHNSTON.

Salisbury township, Lancaster county, Octo. 16.

Pennsylvania Packet, Philadelphia

157.   July 17, 1787 – Maria Magdalena van Beethoven, the mother of Ludwig van Beethoven dies at age 40. Her son, Beethoven, was seventeen at the time.

1788

158.   1788 – Sacagawea was born this year in 1788 in the area of Salmon, Idaho

1789

159. We thought that after the Salem Witch Trials of 1692 we had heard the last of folks accusing others of being witches. Until April of 1789

April 22, 1789 – [England]: *"A poor woman was indicted for witchcraft. The inhabitants of the place were exasperated against her. Some witnesses deposed that they had seen her walk in the air with her feet upwards. Lord Mansfield heard the evidence with great tranquility and perceiving the temper of the people whom it would not have been prudent to irritate, he thus addressed them. 'I do not doubt that his woman has walked in the air, with her feet upwards, since you have all seen it. But, she has the honor to be born in England as well as you and I and consequently cannot be judged but by the laws of the country, nor punished but in proportion as she has violated them. Now I know not one law that forbids walking in the air with the feet upwards. We have all a right to do it with impunity. I see no reason therefore for prosecution and this poor woman may return home when she please."* ~ **Gazette of the United States**

April 30, 1789 George Washington is sworn in as the first President of the United States. John Adams is the first Vice President.

---

160.   Martha Washington becomes the **first** First Lady of the United States on **April 30, 1789**. Although, at the time, the term 'First Lady' had not been coined. Instead, she was often referred to as *'the Lady of the President, Lady Washington,'* or the *President's Lady.*

161.   May 7, 1789 – *"Extensive preparations have been made by the subscribers to the city dancing assemblies, to pay the President the compliment of an inauguration ball. The honored lady of the Chieftain,* *however, had not accompanied her *august husband to New York, but was to follow in a few days.*

The anxiety for her arrival was therefore great, though of course proportionally less than it had been for the President elect himself. But a short time intervened, however, before her approach to Elizabethtown was announced, accompanied by the Lady of Robert Morris, the Senator of Philadelphia.

She was met by the President at Elizabethtown Point, who proceeded thither, with Robert Morris and several other gentlemen of distinction in the barge towed by 13 eminent pilots in handsome white dresses. The passage through the bay presented a brilliant spectacle; a salute was fired from the Battery and on her landing she was welcomed by crowds of citizens, who had assembled to testify their joy.

Upon a platform, handsomely carpeted, and beneath a rich drapery of curtains and banners was placed a damask covered sofa upon which the President and Lady Washington were to be seated. The platform was ascended by a flight of three or four steps. The costume of the gentlemen was prescribed; hair was to be dressed in bags, with two long curls on the sides, with powder and all were to appear and dance with small swords. Each gentleman, on taking a partner to dance was to lead her to the foot of the sofa and make a low obeisance to the President and his Lady and repeat the ceremony before taking their seats after the figure was concluded.

[...] Never was a lady, either in public or private life, more popular than Mrs. Washington and from the moment of her arrival, the most respectful attentions had been paid to her by the principal ladies of the city and by those likewise of celebrity from a distance. A numerous and brilliant collection of ladies consequently graced the saloon with their presence, on the proud occasion. Among the leading circle were:
The lady of his excellency Gov. Clinton
Lady Sterling
Lady Mary Watts
Lady Kitty Duer
La Marchioness de Brehan
Mrs. Langdon
Mrs. Dalton
Mrs. Duane (the Mayoress)
Mrs. Peter Van Brook Livingston
Mrs. Livingston of Clermont
Mrs. Chancellor Livingston

Lady Temple
Madame de Forrest
Mrs. Montgomery
Mrs. Knox
Mrs. Thompson
Mrs. Gerry
Mrs. Edgar
Mrs. McComb
Mrs. Lynch
Mrs. Houston
Mrs. Griffin
Mrs. Provost
Miss Bayards

The whole number of ladies and gentlemen at the affair exceeded three hundred." ~ **National Gazette**

*august usually means 'dignified' in this context.

162.   The position of Vice President of the United States was created. Our first Vice President was John Adams in 1789, making Abigail Adams our **first** "Second Lady".

163.   The following several articles I found in the newspapers of this year, 1789, shows how the media and the public, were immediately interested in every move of the First Lady and not something that developed over time.

. *May 22, 1789 – "The amiable Lady of our beloved President arrived in this place on Tuesday evening and set out early next morning for New York. She was met at Hammond's Ferry by several of our citizens and received by such other demonstrations of affection and respect as her short stay admitted. Fireworks were discharged before and after supper and she was serenaded by an excellent band of music conducted by gentlemen of the town. We shall only add, that, like her illustrious husband, she was cloathed in the manufacture of our country, in which her native goodness and patriotism appeared to the greatest advantage."* ~ **Gazette of the United States**

164. *May 23, 1789* – "*Philadelphia: Yesterday Mrs. Washington arrived here from Mount Vernon. This truly respectable personage was met by a number of the principal ladies and gentlemen of this city (among whom were the President of the State, and the Speaker of the General Assembly) a little beyond Derby-at-Grays Ferry, she partook of an elegant cold collation and from thence was escorted to the residence of Mrs. (Robert) Morris, in Market Street by the troops of light horse, commanded by Captains Miles and Bingham. Her arrival, which was about 2 o'clock P.M., was announced by the ringing of bells and a discharge of thirteen guns from the park of artillery under the direction of Captain Fisher.*

We hear that Mrs. Washington intends to favor her female friends in this city with her company till Monday morning, when she will proceed to join her beloved and justly revered consort at New York, the President of the United States." ~**Gazette of the United States, New York**

165. *May 26, 1789* – "*Philadelphia: Intelligence being received on Thursday last by an express appointed for that purpose that the consort of our illustrious President was on her way from Mount Vernon to New York and would breakfast at Chester next morning. The two city troops of light dragoons paraded early on Friday and marched to form her escort. His Excellency the President of the State and the Honorable Speaker of the Assembly attended by a numerous suite of gentlemen on horseback, preceded the troops and the whole, halting ten miles from the city waited the approach of this much respected personage. While they paid the compliment of military honors due to her exalted rank, they offered still more grateful tribute of heartfelt regard to the amiable virtues, which distinguish and adorn her character. The present occasion recalled the remembrance of those interesting scenes in which, by her presence, she contributed to relieve the cares of our beloved Chief, and to soothe the anxious moments of his military concern. Gratitude marked the recollection and every countenance bespoke the feelings of affectionate respect.*

Seven miles from the city she was met by a brilliant company of ladies, in carriages, who attended her to Gray's Ferry on Schuylkill, where an elegant entertainment of upwards of one hundred covers was prepared at a few hours' notice. The repast being finished, the procession was recommenced and the corps of artillery, being formed on their parade near the city, saluted with a discharge of 13 cannons; the bells were rung and a joyous concourse of citizens welcomed, with affectionate shouts the much respected and beloved Mrs. Washington to Philadelphia.

Mrs. Morris having met her honored guest at Darby, 8 miles from town, conducted her to her house in Market Street, where, taking leave of her escort, Mrs. Washington in the most gracious manner thanked the troops for their polite attention.

Having fixed her departure for yesterday morning the troops paraded with an intention to escort her to Trenton. His Excellency the President of the State, and many gentlemen on horseback attending at ten o'clock the procession moved from Mrs. Morris's house, who, in her own carriage, accompanies Mrs. Washington to New York. The weather proving rainy, she requested that the troops might return and they took a respectful leave of her a few miles from the city.

During her short stay in Philadelphia, the citizens have vied with each other in demonstrations of respectful attachment to this most amiable woman" ~ **Gazette of the United States**

166. May 27, 1789 – *"The Lady of the President of the United States is expected to arrive in this city, on Wednesday or Thursday of this week.*

This morning at 5 o'clock the President set off in his barge, to meet Mrs. Washington at Elizabethtown Point." ~ **Gazette of the U.S.**

NEW-YORK, MAY 30, 1789.

Wednesday arrived in this city from Mount Vernon, Mrs. WASHINGTON, the amiable consort of THE PRESIDENT of the United States. Mrs. Washington from Philadelphia was accompanied by the Lady of Mr. Robert Morris. At Elizabethtown point she was met by the THE PRESIDENT, Mr. Morris, and several other gentlemen of distinction, who had gone there for that purpose.—She was conducted over the bay in the President's Barge, rowed by 13 eminent pilots, in a handsome white dress; on passing the Battery a salute was fired; and on her landing she was welcomed by crowds of citizens, who had assembled to testify their joy on this happy occasion.

167. *May 30, 1789 – "Wednesday arrived in this city from Mount Vernon, Mrs. Washington, the amiable consort of the President of the United States. Mrs. Washington, from Philadelphia was accompanied by the Lady of Mr. Robert Morris. At Elizabethtown point she was met by the President, Mr. Morris and several other gentlemen of distinction who had gone there for that purpose. She was over the bay in the Presidents barge, rowed by 13 eminent pilots in a handsome white* *dress. On passing the Battery a salute was fired and on her landing she was welcomed by crowds of citizens who had assembled to testify their joy on this happy occasion."* **Gazette of the United States, New York**

168. Women's Protest:

August 13, 1789 – "At Lisle, there has been a commotion, marked by the singularity of its having been effected by women! The cause was this: the Canons of St. Peter's Church are, by their charter, bound to distribute one-fourth part of their tithes to the poor. The terms have not been complied with for the last forty-nine years. In the present distressful season, an application was made to these sons of the church for some relief. Every circumstance that could excite compassion was laid before them but, in vain. In consequence of this on the morning of 21st of July **about 400 countrywomen surrounded the cathedral and clamored loudly against these unfeeling monsters.**

The clerical gentlemen, not trusting wholly to their faith, called in the grenadiers, who dispersed this female mob.

The ladies, however, not dismayed by this defeat, returned the next day to the charge with a reinforcement of near a thousand women and forced the sheriffs of the city to distribute 625 pounds among them." ~ The Bath Chronicle, Avon, England

169. August 25, 1789, in Fredericksburg, Mary Ball Washington, the mother of President George Washington, dies. Here is the obituary as it was printed in the Gazette of the United States on September 9, 1789:

September 3, 1789 – "Fredericksburg (August 27). On Tuesday, the 25th, died at her house in this town, Mrs. Mary Washington, aged 82 years, the venerable mother of the illustrious President of the United States, after a long and painful indisposition which she bore with uncommon patience. Tho' the pious tear of duty, affection and esteem is due to the memory of so revered a character, yet our grief must be greatly alleviated from the consideration that she is relieved from all the pitiful infirmities attendant on an extreme old age. It is usual when virtuous and conspicuous persons quit this terrestial abode to publish an elaborate, panegyric on their characters. Suffice it to say, she conducted herself through this transatory lite with virtue, prudence and christianity worthy; the mother of the greatest hero that ever adorned the annals of history."

170. Women's March on Versailles was one of the early women's protests over the high price and scarcity of bread. On October 5, 1789 in Paris a very large group of women ascended on the Paris marketplace to demand bread to feed their families. This is just one article on how this event was reported to the public:

"On Monday morning the general alarm of the people as to the intentions of the court, and scarcity of bread, brought on a gradual insurrection in every quarter of Paris. The women flocked in the most riotous manner to the Palace de Louis XIV. They were armed with stronger weapons than they could wield and as they advanced, pressed every woman they met with into their service.

[...] A sufficient guard was then ordered for the defense of the city. [...] The women appeared more savage than the men, marching toward Versailles, storming the palace gates, calling for bread.

The whole Royal family began to be alarmed for their personal safety. The Life Guard fired on the women who became furious and assisted as they were, victorious. Five young noblemen were immediately sacrificed to their vengeance; one run through the body, one hung and a third cut to pieces while two were beheaded. The Marquis de la Fayette came in time to save the lives of about twenty others.

Tuesday morning many of the mob returned from Versailles with the heads of the two officers on pikes while walking through the streets of Paris.

To understand what has happened requires a knowledge of the French character and of the human heart; a reference must be made to a long system of slavery and of cruel and miserable policy for millions in this country have endured in order to account for the manner in which the sudden rising of many thousands of women, who wanted for bread, assembling as if by instinct in the corners of the city and committing acts of mad barbarity on those who compose of it, forcing themselves into the assembly of the nation." ~ Hartford Courant, Connecticut, December 7, 1789

171.   November 21, 1789 – (National Assembly, France) "*Discourse delivered at the National Assembly on the 7th of September, 1789 by the female citizens who came to make an offering of their jewels and other ornaments as a voluntary distribution towards the discharge of the public debts.*

The regeneration of the state is a work committed to the National Representatives. In order to enable the Senate to fulfill a vow that was made by Camillus to Apollo before the capture of Vieum, the Roman ladies made a voluntary offering of their ornaments to the Republic. But, no vows can be more sacred than engagements contracted with the creditors of the state, the public debt should be scrupulously discharged, but the means should be rendered easy to the people.

It is in that view that several citizens; wives or daughters of artists, came to offer to this august National Assembly those ornaments which they would blush to wear when patriotism bids them sacrifice them to the public good. What woman is there, worthy of the title of citizen, who would not prefer to the insipid parade of vanity, the inexpressible pleasure of converting the ornaments of her person to so excellent a use?" ~ Gazette of the United States, New York

1790

By 1790 approximately 2.5 million people, in thirteen states had firmly come together to form the Thirteen American Colonies. They included:

Delaware, Pennsylvania, New Jersey, Georgia, Connecticut, Massachusetts, Maryland, South Carolina, New Hampshire, Virginia, New York, North Carolina and Rhode Island.

172. January 15, 1790 – Patriotic Women. *"The late act of patriotism exhibited by the French ladies must place them in an elevated degree of estimation. Modern times have certainly produced many instances of this sublime virtue, which rank as highly as any of those that have received the just plaudit of antiquity.*

During the American War, the patriotism of the fair sex was evinced in a heroic self-denial of tea, from which the dispute originated with Britain. They likewise associated in considerable bodies and with the first female characters of the state at their head, employed themselves in making up linen for the use of those assertors of the public liberty who were engaged in the field. We find our charming countrywomen also, on some occasions, have been tremblingly alive to the sufferings of the manufacturers of this kingdom, and materially to have alleviated the general distress by appearing in the native fabrics only. In the sister kingdom, 1742, during the calamities of Maria Theresa, mother to the present Emperor of Germany, the British ladies entered into resolutions to dispose of their jewels, in order to relieve her from some of her embarrassments and actually subscribed 100,000 pounds to secure a foreign Princess of whom they knew nothing but her misfortunes." ~ **The Pennsylvania Packet, Philadelphia**

173. *January 21, 1790* – "(Boston)   *"It can be contended on the principles of policy and liberality that the present custom in the world, especially in America, of excluding women from any share in legislation is both unjust and detrimental. It is certainly unjust to exclude from any share in government one half of those who considered as equals of the males are obliged to subject to laws they have no share in making! And that policy is not consulted in it, may be reasoned from experience. Witness the glorious reigns of Elizabeth and Ann of England, both of immortal fame. The late Empress of Germany, Maria Theresa, the quondam poor Queen of Hungary, afterwards elevated to the highest dignities and dominion which Europe could afford. Witness all the Empresses of all the Russia's, and the late famous Elizabeth, of the same rank, honor and dignity. And the present reigning Queen of Portugal who seems to reign in the hearts of her subjects."* ~ **Pennsylvania Packet, Philadelphia.**

174.   *February 11, 1790* – *"Miss Cantelo is not only engaged as the first woman at the oratorios at Covent-Garden, but also at the professional concert."* ~ **The Bath Chronicle, Bath, Avon, England**

> Miſs Cantelo is not only engaged as firſt woman at the orato-
> rios at Covent-Garden, but alſo at the Profeſſional Concert.

175. *February 11, 1790* – *"LACE WAREHOUSE, Bath, England: Elizabeth Johnson returns her grateful acknowledgments to her friends, and the ladies in general, for the many favors conferred on her since she opened the above warehouse and respectfully informs them that she has just received from her manufactory in Salisbury a fresh and very beautiful assortments of laces and edgings of the newest patterns.*

She flatters herself that by means of her own manufactory and her extensive connections in that line of business she has the advantage of offering to the ladies not only a greater variety of elegant and fashionable laces and edgings of all sorts than is usually to be met with, but to render the on such terms as to merit a continuance of that very liberal encouragement with which she has been honored. N. B. Lace mended in the neatest manner and point and brussels new grounded." ~ **The Bath Chronicle, Bath, Avon, England**

176. Bill HR 41, U.S. Patent Act of 1790.. Enacted on April 10, 1790. It was this Act that legally allowed women to file a patent in their own name here in the United States. Previous to this official Act, women were not allowed to file for a patent here in the United States.

Sec. 1. *B*E it enacted by the Senate and House of Representatives of the United States of America, in Congress assembled, That upon the petition of any person or persons to the Secretary of State, setting forth that he, she or they, hath or have invented or discovered any useful art, manufacture, engine, machine, or device, or any improvement upon, or in some art, manufacture, engine, machine, invention or device, not before known or used within the United States, and praying that a patent may be granted therefor, the said Secretary of State shall make out an advertisement, to be inserted by the peti-

*Notably that it states, "he, she or they…".

  You will recall item number 43 of this book, the year being 1715 whereas Sybilla Righton Masters who lived here, in Colonial America, received a patent, actually two patents. Her first was for the machine that made grits and then she filed for a second patent for a new process of making hats and bonnets. Since Colonial America was under British rule in 1715 she was granted her request for these patents under British Parliament.

  The popular opinion is that the first patent filed in the United States by a woman was Mary Kies in 1809 due to the fact this was the first patent filed by a female after the U.S. Patent Act of 1790 and I suppose,, that it was, in fact, the first patent granted to a woman by the United States Patent Office. Each person can decide for themselves which is first if it matters at all. But let us not forget to give Sybil her credit where credit is due on her patents so very long ago.

  Whoa, not so fast. But wait, there was also a woman named Hannah Wilkinson Slater who, three years after the Patent Act of 1790, in 1793, filed for a patent for her new process of making thread. According to Encyclopedia Britannica it is Hannah Slater, and not Mary Kies who is the first woman to receive a patent in the United States. The name that the patent was issued in being Mrs. Samuel Slater and not Hannah Slater. Who was first, second and third will depend on your interpretation and level of technicality you wish to place on each patent.

[blogs.britannica.com/2011/03/10-key-dates-womens-history-early-modern-period]

177. September 1, 1790 – "(New York) On Monday, at ten o'clock a.m. the President of the United States and his Lady departed from this city. They embarked at Mr. McCombs Wharf in the Presidents barge and crossed the north river to Powles Hook. The Governor, the Chief Justice and executive officers of the U.S., the corporation of the city, gentlemen of the clergy, officers of the militia and a number of other respectable citizens attended by the Sheriff, Marshalls and Constables accompanied them to the place of embarkation where they took a solemn and affecting adieu." ~ Gazette of the United States

178. *November 4, 1790 –*

"**Acts Before the British Parliament:**

An Act to limit and regulate Female Boarding Schools and that none shall be qualified unless the Mistress have a certificate signed by the Bishop of the Diocese, the Curate and Rector of the parish, and majority of the Protestant inhabitants.

An Act totally to clear our streets of nightwalking prostitutes, and for the due regulation of bagnios.

An Act for imposing a duty on bachelors and maiden women after a certain age.

An Act for badging the carriages and wearing apparel of women of the town, that virtue may be outwardly distinguished from vice.

An Act to prevent the intercourse of black men and white women, and black women and white men, which intercourse has of late years enormously increased." ~ The Times, London, England

179. **Newspaper commentary . I hope this exchange, in the year 1790, of four women, overheard by the newspapers reporter, delights you as much as it did me. I find it interesting to know what women were talking and thinking about years ago in another time.**

[Commentary]: *"I happened lately to be in the company of several young ladies where the following very curious conversation took place.*

Girl 1: I long for a change of affairs! We shall expunge the odious obey from the wedding ceremony. Then, my girls, we shall first be absolute mistresses of our houses and then in very short time govern the state also. We shall in this western hemisphere set up a female empire that shall laugh at all the male government in the world.

Girl 2: My dear girl, let me kiss you for that greatness of soul. Oh, may the glorious day soon dawn, when our sex shall be delivered from an ignominious slavery of 6000 years. A slavery founded upon the story of our first mother's eating a forbidden apple. A slavery exercised by pedants, blockheads, drones, drunkards, bigots, and rakes, over the far more virtuous, sensible and lovely part of the human species.

In fifty quarto volumes of ancient and modern history, you will not find fifty illustrious female names; heroes, statesmen, divines, philosophers, artists are all of the masculine gender. And pray what have they done during this long period of usurpation? Busy they have been with a witness: They have written ten thousand unintelligible books. They have labored 1000 years to establish erroneous systems and worked hard again for another 1000 years to pull them down. They have been cutting each other's throats all over the globe, and murdered at least one hundred millions in quarrels about idols, titles, gold lace, nutmeg and rum. They have disputed for many centuries about the best form of government, without producing one good pattern. I boldly affirm, not one, not even in this county because the federal constitution has the great defect of being too good, that is, of supporting more virtue in the people than they really have; of supporting them wise, generous, brave, when they cannot see their true interest, when they love self and hate martial exercises.

Girl 1: I am exceedingly pleased, my dear, you're your congenial sentiments, and hope that we have 100,000 sisters in the United States. I anticipate the glorious day when American ladies shall be commanders, presidents of congress, ambassadors, governors, secretaries of state, professors, judges, preachers. When the golden age of the poets and the millennium of the Christians shall be realized in America.

Girl 3: Yet ladies, you must in the execution of this splendid plan, employ the men, at least in subordinate parts.

Girl 1: Yes, yes, we will make them hewers of wood and drawers of water, they shall cook for us, make our shoes, knit stockings, and wash our linen. We shall perhaps employ some of them as pioneers and butlers in our camps, mere quill drivers in the petty offices, door keepers, messengers, sextons and so forth.

Girl 3: But will they submit to this inferiority?

Girl 2: Inferior minds will be fitted for inferior stations. We shall keep the sword and the purse in our own hands. We shall moreover keep them ignorant and from infancy bend their mind to servility.

Girl 3: But, after all, is not woman made for man? And would you be the wife of such a pusillanimous creature? If not, how would you preserve this noble race of females and the grand empire you talk of.

Girl 1: I confess you puzzle me. However, we must pick out the least defective males, or else import from Europe some of their best men, cost what it will.

Girl 3: This would still be a very partial supply. Nine in ten of the women must die old maids.

Girl 2: It is so. We must make that use of the men which nature intended. I hope also, that this necessary evil will not spoil the offspring. Because the great Linneus has proved that we derive the mental part from our mothers. Admitting that the bodies of our children should be the worse for the imbecility of their fathers, we can harden them by cold baths and exercise.

Girl 4: My dear friends, your schemes are utopian. The laws of Providence are immutable. Man must do the rough work of society. Woman shines in the tender cares and elegant arts of domestic life. Let us carry a counter-petition to Congress, signed by ten thousand fair Americans. Let us boldly declare that we will never marry a man who cannot, in case of need, protect us and our children.

The ladies proceeded in sketching this petition. It was arranged within an hour and is now circulating over the country for subscription. I shall shortly give you a copy. Your friend, C." ~ **Gazette of the United States, New York**

179. Etta Lubina Johanna Palm d'Aelders was a Dutch spy and feminist. She addressed the French National Convention on December 30, 1790 reciting the 'Discourse on the Injustice of the Laws in Favor of Men at the Expense of Women' She also was one of

the founding members of the very first female only organization in France. Her biography was written in 1926, 'Etta Palm een Hollandse Parisienne 1743-1799'.

1791

Vermont was admitted into the Union March 4, 1791 becoming the 14th state.

180. *February 28, 1791 –* *"On Thursday the 20th, a free mulatto woman was accidentally shot in Annapolis by a lad who was amusing himself with a gun. The gun, we learn, had for some time been standing loaded in the store which this unfortunate woman was entering when the youth, unaware that it was charged, drew the trigger, which lodged the contents in her body and put a period to her existence on the spot. This melancholy catastrophe, it is hoped, will prove a serious lesson to those who inconsiderately and wantonly sport with guns." ~* Hartford Courant, Connecticut

181. The bestselling book in American literature, Charlotte Temple, written by author Susanna Rowson, is published in 1791. This book remains the bestselling book of the times until Harriet Beecher Stowes
'Uncle Tom's Cabin' is published in 1851.

Susanna Rowson was born in 1762 in Portsmouth, England but the family almost immediately moved to the America's. The ship did not even make it to the docks; the ship becoming grounded and considered shipwrecked some distance out the crew and passengers were stuck on the ship until rescued days later.

With the American Revolutionary War going on, Susanna's father was immediately placed under house arrest. Following a prisoner exchange in 1778, the family was sent to live in Halifax, Nova Scotia, and then back to England. Their property in America was seized and the family found themselves living in poverty. Susanna would go on to become a famous and beloved writer and **the first woman geographer when she published the first human geography textbook, 'Rowson's Abridgement of Universal Geography' in 1805.**

182. 1791 - The Haitian Revolution took place between the years of 1791 and 1804. Women played a great part in the revolution in which the black slaves ultimately ousted the French from power on the island and virtually eradicated all whites from the island. This most certainly included all white women as the argument was that if white women were spared they could continue to give birth to more whites. As a result of the Haitian Revolution, Haiti became the first country to abolish slavery.

Many, many women literally fought in the war for their freedom but remain anonymous. I wanted to highlight at least a few of these brave women that we are aware of.

183. Cecil Fatiman was a black Haitian vodou priestess, sometimes referred to as a mambo. Her notoriety stems from her part in the vodou ceremony at Bois Caiman which is thought to be the starting point of the Haitian Revolution. Bois Caiman is where enslaved blacks met to plan the very first insurrection. (B:1791-D:1883)

184. Suzanne Belair was a Lieutenant during the Haitian Revolution, fighting in several conflicts. (B:1781-D:1802) Considered a hero, she was featured on the ten-gourd banknote in 2004.

2008 Haitian banknote
featuring Sanité Bélair

185. Catherine Flon sewed the first Haitian Flag in May of 1803

Liberte ou La Mort means: 'Freedom or Death'.

186. Marie Jeanne Lamartiniere served in the Haitian Army during the revolution. She was known for being fearless and courageous fighting alongside the men with her rifle and sword. She was celebrated with her likeness on a commemorative postage stamp in 1954:

187. It was 1791 when Mary Woolstoncraft published 'The Rights of Women'. Mary is the mother of Mary Shelley, author of Frankenstein.

188. **September 14, 1791** French activist, feminist and playwright **Olympe de Gouges** publishes 'Declaration Of The Rights Of Woman And Of The Female Citizen'.

Kentucky officially becomes a state on June 1, 1792.

1792

189. **In Royal News**: *January 9, 1792 – "The languor of a long sitting at the play on Wednesday night; perhaps, also some shock coming with the information of the melancholy accident which occurred there, rendered her Majesty slightly indisposed yesterday and the care of Dr. Dundas prevented her from leaving her apartments.*
We are happy, however, to learn, upon inquiry at Buckingham House, that her Majesty was sufficiently recovered as to be able to set off this morning for Windsor." **~ The Caledonian Mercury, Edinburgh, Scotland**

*This is referring to Queen Charlotte, consort to King George III. It was during the reign of George III and Charlotte that Buckingham Palace was purchased in 1762, at that time known as the Queen's House. Queen Charlotte also purchased Frogmore House in Windsor Park in 1792 as a country retreat. Queen Charlotte's music master was Johann Christian Bach, the 11th son of the famous composer Johann Sebastian Bach. An 8-year-old youngster named Mozart performed for the Queen.

Queen Charlotte was very engaged in her community and she founded several orphanages. In 1809 she was named Patron of the General Lying-In Hospital, eventually renamed the Queen's Hospital and, today, still in service is called The Queen Charlottes and Chelsea Hospital.

The Regency Bill of 1765 created a new statute that stated if the King should become unable to rule, Queen Charlotte would become Regent. This was altered with the Regency Bill of 1778 changing it to name the Prince of Wales as Regent assuming such an event.

[royal.uk/queen-charlotte]

190.
On April 13, 1792 – **Portugal Black Women Protest** : *"The want of common sewers in Lisbon before its destruction by the late earthquake made the carrying human odor out of houses in large pots a great employment for black women; many of whom being slaves maintained poor widows with families of orphans by such work. But a tax being laid of a third part of such earning and some duties in that country being received in kind.*

When the day came on which the tax payments of tax commenced, all the black women went with their pots to the palace door, where they told the soldiers on guard they were come to pay his Majesty's tax. This as may well be supposed caused a crowd to assemble, the consequences of which were much mirth and some disturbance.

They were civilly desired to go off quietly with their loads, which they refused till the King sent them an order to depart on his royal promise that the tax should be abolished as it immediately was." ~ **Aurora General Advertiser**

191.

I wanted to include this "Letter To The Editor" to show that not all men shared the same view of women. How women are viewed is very important in understanding our equality or lack of equality during certain times in history. Men and women alike were reading the occasional article(s) such as the one below in the newspapers during the late 1700s.

December 26, 1792 – Letter To The Editor: *"That women greatly influence the habits and manners of men the history of most civilized countries as well as our own experience will sufficiently prove nay that they often give impressions which continue during life, the observations of every unprejudiced observer will equally substantiate. It will not be denied that an intercourse with our sex polishes the manners, and gives a decency to the minds of men. If such is their influence, I am not wrong in supposing that they are capable and very often give a lift to our political complexion. The superior light in which you have been accustomed to view yourselves, may make this opinion of difficult admission but on reflection it will be found that the secret power which we have over you, enables us to fashion you lords of the creation as we please. It is fiercely necessary to resort to times past to prove my position. The history of France will furnish ample testimony in my favor, not only that women have fashioned, but that they have actually governed men; perhaps the cause of the revolution of France may be traced to that government. The Earl of Chesterfield supposed that women gave me a currency and the history of some of the ancient republics informs us that women formed some of their most renowned patriots. It is a trite saying that a man must ask his wife if he shall be rich. I will extend this further and say that a man must ask our sex if he shall be free. The great influence which fashion has may be justly termed tyranny, and there are fashionable opinions as well as fashions in dress, and that we direct fashion is incontrovertible. If then a fashion is then introduced which may serve to lessen the independence of the human mind by teaching it a humility repugnant to republican principles, am I not just in the inference that we form your political characters. That we can hold out liberty or slavery to you? So jealous is the government of China that the customs, manners, and fashions of the present day have been from time immemorial and are preserved with an almost religious veneration, left a change in them might produce a revolution in their political belief. Ought we not to have the same jealousy with regard to our government, and, if possible, stifle any practices which favor of distinction and inequality, lest we lay a foundation for a change in our political order? The above remarks suggested themselves to my mind on reading some reflections in your paper under the different signatures of Mirabeau and Condorcet. The remarks of those writers are but too just, but they have not struck the evil at its root. I conceive that they should have resorted to us as leading instruments in such anti-republican distinctions. Witness the drawing room!!*

No character or place ought to be so sacred in a republican government as to be above criticism. Infallibility are royal qualities, which slaves only can comprehend. It is the unalienable prerogative of freemen to scrutinize the conduct of their rulers, and if derogatory to just and equal principles it ought to meet their severest reprehension. To elevate any character, however meritorious, beyond the level of scrutiny, is to establish a precedent, big with the most destructive consequences. It is to lay out the turnpike of slavery. It might be considered as an invasion of female rights for you gentlemen to comment upon the conduct of women, but for one of the same sex to do it will abate a little of the censure. Mine has been the talk and I trust that my fair countrywomen will not persist in giving currency to opinions, destructive of equality the vital principle of republicanism. Let us fashion men to virtue, but not to the servility and adulation of royalty. Let us reverence merit in whatever form or station it may appear to us but let it be the reverence of dignified and independent minds. Let us display our charms to show our individual freedom and consequence, but let us beware of becoming satellites, lest our revolutions should be made permanent, and we be deprived of the power of receding. In a free government every man is a king, every woman is a queen. Each should preserve the individual sovereignty guaranteed by our constitution that ALL MEN ARE BORN EQUALLY FREE. To homage any one is to destroy the equality which constitutes the essense of our sovereignty, and is a degradation of freemen." ~ Aurora General Advertiser, Philadelpha, PA

1793

192.

1793 - Dolley Madison, (future First Lady), married her first husband, John Todd in 1790. Together they had two sons but this year, in 1793 during a yellow fever outbreak her husband and one son dies from the disease.

193.

1793 - January 10, 1793 – **Women Volunteers**. *"French National Convention. Letter from the Commissioners to the Army of the *Pyrennees. The battalions are raising with great alacrity. Beds being wanted, the female citizens offered to work at them and what could not have been done by the contractor in three months, will be finished in a fortnight. The barracks being in want of repair, the women offered to bring tools and work gratuitously."* ~ Aurora General Advertiser, Philadelphia, PA

*Pyrennees is a mountain range separating France and Spain

The Fugitive Slave Act of 1793 is enacted.

This act guaranteed the right of a slaveholder to recover an escaped slave.

---

194. In October of 1793 the trial of Maria Antoinette begins.

'ortrait of Marie Antoinette, 1775

Maria Antonia Josepha Johanna was born on November 2, 1755. When she was age 14 in 1770, she married Louis Auguste, heir apparent to the French throne. This made her Dauphine of France. Four years later her husband ascended to the throne as Louis XVI which made her the Queen.

After a tumultuous reign and four children Louis XVI was executed by the guillotine on January 21, 1793. The trial of Marie Antoinette will begin in October of this same year, 1793. The accusations against her were printed in the newspaper

October 21, 1793 – "Trial of the Queen. *Accusation and Interrogatory of Maria Antoinette of Austria, Queen of France.*

Being interrogated as to her names, surnames, age, qualities, place of birth and abode, answered, That her name is Marie Antoinette Lorraine of Austria, aged about 38 years, widow of the King of France, born at Vienna, finding herself at the time of her arrest in the place of the sitting of the National Assembly.

The Act of Accusation was read as follows:

Antoine Quentin Fouquier, Public Accuser of the criminal revolutionary tribunal established at Paris, by a decree of the National Convention of the 10th of March, 1793, second year of the Republick, without any recourse to the Tribunal of Cessation, in virtue of the power given him by the 11th article of another decree of the convention of April 5, following, stating that the Public Accuser of the said tribunal is authorized to arrest, pursue and judge upon the denunciation of the constituted authorities or of the citizens:

That by a decree of the convention, of 1st of August, last, Marie Antoinette, widow of Louis Capet, has been brought before the Revolutionary Tribunal, as accused of conspiring against France. That by another decree of the convention of Oct 3, if has been decreed that the Revolutionary Tribunal should occupy itself without delay and without interruption on the trial; that the public accuser received the papers concerning the widow Capet, on the 19th and 20th of the first month of the second decade, commonly called 11th and 12th of October of the present month. That an examination being made of all the pieces transmitted by the public accuser, it appears that, like Messaline, Brunchant, Freaigonde, and Medicis, who were formerly qualified with the titles of Queens of France, whose names have ever been odious, and will never be effaced from the page of history.

Marie Antoinette, widow of Louis Capet, has, since her abode in France, been the scourge and the blood-sucker of the French. That even before the happy revolution which gave the French people their sovereignty, she had political correspondence with a man called the King of Bohemia and Hungary. That this correspondence was contrary to the interests of France; that not content with acting in concert with the brothers of Louis Capet, and the infamous and execrable Calonne, at that time Minister of the Finances, of having squandered the finances of France, the fruit of the sweat of the people, in a dreadful manner, to satisfy inordinate pleasures and to pay the agents of her criminal intrigues, it is notorious that she has at different times transmitted millions to the Emperor, which served him, and still supports him to sustain a war against the republic. That it is by such excessive plunder, that she has at length exhausted the national treasury.

That since the revolution, the widow has not for a moment withheld criminal intelligence and correspondence with foreign powers, and in *the interior of the republic, by agents devoted to her, whom she subsidized and caused to be paid out of the treasury of the ci-devant Civil Lift; that at various epochs she has employed every maneuver that she thought consistent with her perfidious views to bring about a counter-revolution; first having under pretext of a necessary reunion between the *ci-devant gardes-du-corps, and the officers and soldiers of the regiment of Flanders contrived a repast between these two corps on the 1st of October 1789 which degenerated into an absolute orgy as she desired, and during the course of which, the agents of the widow Capet perfectly seconded her counter-revolutionary projects; brought the greater part of the guests in the moment of inebriety, to sing songs expressive of their most entire devotion to the throne and the most marked aversion for the people. Having excited them insensibly to wear the white cockade and to tread the national cockade under foot, and of having authorized by her presence all the counter revolutionary excesses, particularly in encouraging the women who accompanied her, to distribute these white cockades among the guests and having, on the 4th, testified the most immoderate joy at what passed during these orgies.*

Secondly: Having in concert with Louis Capet directed to be distributed very plentifully throughout the kingdom publications of a counter revolutionary nature, some of which were pretended to have been published by the conspirators on the other side of the Rhine, such as Petitions to the Emigrants, Reply of the Emigrants, Emigrants to the People, the shortest Follies are the Best, the Order of March and The Return of the Emigrants, and other such writings of having even carried her persidy and dissimulation to such a height as to have circulated writings in which she herself is described in very unfavorable colors in order to cloak the imposture; thereby to make it to be believed to Foreign Powers that she was extremely ill-treated by Frenchmen, to instigate them to go to war with France.

We find it impossible to proceed with giving a detail of the different charges which run to a prodigious length; we shall therefore content ourselves with presenting the public with a short abstract of the charges on which the trial turned.

Marie Antoinette was further accused that being brought to Paris, she immediately began to intrigue with the members of the legislature and held nightly meetings with them.

That she was accessary in getting bad ministers appointed in order that her views might be assisted.

That her creatures were placed in all the public offices, men who were known to be conspirators to liberty.

That she was accessary in bribing the members of the legislative assembly to declare war against the emperor, her brother.

That she gave intelligence to the enemy of the plans of the campaign as soon as they were determined on by the council which was the cause of many failures which the French arms experienced.

That she combined with her agents in plotting the overthrow of the constitution on the 10th day of August 1792.

That on the 9th of the same month, she got a number of Swiss guards into the Tuileries and encouraged them to make cartouches and animated Louis Capet to order his soldiers to fire.

That the Civil War which now rages in France, has been produced by her intrigues.

That Marie Antoinette is such an adept in all sorts of crimes that forgetting her situation of mother, she committed indecencies with her own son too shocking to mention.

She has dilapidated and lavished the finances of the nation in concert with the execrable Calonne by causing to be transmitted to the Emperor several millions which still serve to carry on the war against France.

With having in imitation of Brunehaud and De Medicis, who also called themselves Queens of France, conspired against the liberty of the French Nation.

With having sought to starve the people in 1789.

With having excited the murders of October 5 and 6th.

With having in concert with Bailly and La Fayette, caused the patriots to be butchered in the Champ de Mars.

With having prevailed upon the Swiss to fire on the people on the 10th of August.

With having like another Agrippina, forgotten that she was a mother in order to commit incest with her son.

Marie Antoinette heard the reading of the Act of Accusation without seeming to be in the least moved.

President: What is your name?
Queen: Marie Antoinette of Lorraine and Austria
President: Your quality?
Queen: I am the widow of Louis Capet, King of the French.

Laurent Lecointre, the first witness, formerly Chief of Division of the National Guard of Versailles, and at present a member of the National Convention, related the historical occurrences of the 5th and 6th of October and from his relation it appeared that the ci-devant guardes du corps or life-guards, were the first aggressors. Lecointre spoke also, though not as an ocular witness of the nocturnal riot which was occasioned Oct 1st at Versailles, by the late King's life guards in the Hall of the Opera. Marie Antoinette repaired to that banquet; she applauded the conduct of the guards and also visited the regiment of Nassau and the Chasleurs of Trois Eveches, who were quartered in the Orangerie of the Gardens of Versailles.

Queen: I repaired, I must own, with my husband and his children to the Hall of the Opera House but I did not see that the national cockade was trod underfoot. It is false that I ever spoke to the soldiers of the regiment of Nassau or to the Chaffeurs of Trois Eveches.
President: What did you say to the life guards when you appeared at that orgy?
Queen: I applauded that banquet, because it was to have produced the union of the life guards with the National Guards.
Public Accuser: Have you not holden secret councils at the house of the ci-devant Duchess of Polignac? Councils at which the ci-devant French Princes assisted, and in which after having discussed the fate of the Empire you gave yourself up to the infamous pleasures of debauchery?
Queen: All the state affairs were discussed in council and no where else. I have no knowledge of the rest of this assertion.
Judge Did not your husband communicate his designs to you when he invested the Hall of the Representatives of the people with troops?
Queen: My husband reposed his confidence in me; he communicated to me the speech which he was to have made on that occasion. He had, in other respects, no bad intentions.
Judge: What use have you made of the immense sums wich you have been entrusted with?
Queen: No enormous sum has been entrusted to me. The accounts of my household will prove what use has been made of all I have received.
Judge: How did the family of the Polignacs who were so poor at first, grow so rich.
Queen: That family held offices at court which were very lucrative."

*ci-devant: those who refused to be a part of the new social order in France after the revolution.

October 27, 1793 – *"Execution of the Queen of France: Of this melancholy event, some particulars are given in the Paris papers of the 17th.*

The once all powerful and beautiful Marie Antoinette, consort of the unfortunate Louis, King of France, the daughter, sister and aunt, of Emperors, was brought like the meanest malefactor from the prison of the conciergerie, and placed at the criminal bar of the Revolutionary Tribunal.

The execution took place on Wednesday the 16th.

All the National Guards in the several sections of Paris were arms and Henriot the Commandant in Chief attended the Queen in a private coach with a guard of cavalry to the place of execution.

Nothing like sorrow or pity for the Queen's fate was shown by the people who lined the streets through which she had to pass. On her arrival at the place de la Revolution she was helped out of the carriage and ascended the scaffold with seeming composure. She was accompanied by a priest, who discharged the office of confessor and gave her absolution before she was fixed to the fatal machine.

She was in a half mourning dress, evidently not adjusted with much attention. Her hands were tied behind her back. She looked around, apparently without much terror. Her body being then bent forward by the machine. The axe was let down and at once separated the head from the body. After the head was displayed by the executioner, three young women were observed dipping their handkerchiefs in the streaming blood of the deceased Queen. They were taken into custody." ~ The Observer, London, England

195. Olympe de Gouges dies by the guillotine on November 3, 1793. You will remember Ms. De Gouges from item #188 when in September of 1791 she published the book, 'Declaration of the Rights of Women'.

Born Marie Gouze on May 7, 1748 Olympe would become a French playwright and political activist fighting for women's rights and the end of slavery. She was executed for her verbal and written attacks on the government.

prifoners now confined is 3210. A woman, of the name of *Olympe Gouges*, has been *guillotinea* for having c written writings againſt the Sovereignty of the People.

The Evening Mail, London, England, Nov 11, 1793

196.

Before we present Madame Roland's obituary due to her unfortunate demise on the guillotine first let me introduce her to you.

  Marie Jeanne Manon Roland de la Platiere was born on March 17, 1754 in Paris. She became more involved in political influence in 1792 when her husband became Minister of the Interior. The following obit goes into more details of the life she lived.

November 08, 1793 – "*Madame Roland, who was wife to the Minister of that name, has fallen a sacrifice to the guillotine. Perhaps Madame Roland was the most extraordinary woman that this or any other age has produced. During the administration of her husband, she was the author of all those papers signed by him, which for composition, brilliancy of language, and sentiments of patriotism are unrivalled. To the enthusiasm of a spirited reformist, she added a degree of firmness that gave weight to her decisions, and made her company sought after by all the moderns of Paris. She had her regular levees of statesmen, and consulted as though she were the Prime Minister of State. Courteous in her demeanor, and easy in her manners, though her extreme good judgment and sense, awed her inferiors into respectful silence, yet, she had those means of conciliation in her power that never failed to render her mistress of the principles and the object of those by whom she was consulted. Whenever Roland gave a political dinner, his lady always presided for it was she alone that raised him to that situation, which, at length, proved fatal to this great woman. In consequence of his having attached himself to the weakest party. Madame Roland was in her 46th year when her neck was submitted to the fatal guillotine. In her prime of life, she was considered a beautiful woman.*

A letter from Vienna, dated Nov 2, says the first afflicting news of the dreadful murder of the Queen of France arrived here from Brussels on the 26th. Yesterday, agreeably to a determination of our ministry, the court went into mourning for her Majesty, the deceased Queen of France, Arch Duchess of Austria, the Princess Royal of Hungary and Bohemia. Out of 46 days, 32 shall be deep mourning. It still remains quite fresh in our memory that Marie Antoinette, at her departure from Vienna, was almost drowned in tears. Arrived at Lintz on her way to Paris, she still insisted to return to Vienna and even at Augsburg, she repeatedly cried out, 'anywhere but to France!' The Imperial Resident there had much to do to persuade the favorite daughter of Maria Theresa, to continue her journey to that unfortunate capital." ~ **The Ipswich Journal, Suffolk, England**

"*Madame Roland's last letter to her daughter, her only child written during her imprisonment and a short time before her execution. This great and celebrated woman, wife to the minister of the home department, suffered on the scaffold during the reign of Robespierre, in France.*

(In a letter dated October 18, 1793) To My Daughter: I do not know, my dear girl, whether I shall be allowed to see or to write to you again. Remember Your Mother. In these few words is contained the best advice I can give you. You have seen me happy in fulfilling my duties, and in giving assistance to those who are in distress. It is the only way of being so.

You have seen me tranquil in misfortune and in confinement, because I was free from remorse, and because I enjoyed the pleasing recollections that good actions leave behind. This also is the only means of supporting the evils of life and the vicissitudes of fortune.

Perhaps, as I hope, you are not fated to undergo trials so severe as mine, but there are others against which you ought to be equally on your guard. Propriety of conduct, and occupation are the best preservatives against every danger and necessity as well as prudence require you to attend seriously to your studies.

Be worthy of your parents. They leave you great examples to follow and if you are careful to avail yourself of them, your existence will be useless to mankind.

Farewell, my beloved child, you who drew life from my bosom, and whom I wish to impress with all my sentiments. The time will come when you will be better able to judge of the efforts, I make at this moment to repress the violent emotions which your dear image excites. I press you to my heart."

To her servant she wrote the following:

"To my faithful servant Fleury, My dear Fleury, you, whose friendship, services and attachments have been so grateful to me for these 13 years past, receive my embraces and my farewell. Preserve the remembrance of what I was. It will console you for what I suffer. The good go on to glory, when they descend to the tomb. My sorrows are about to terminate; lay aside yours, and think of the peace which I am about to enjoy and which nobody in future will be able to disturb. Tell my Agatha, that I carry with me to the grave, the satisfaction of being beloved by her from my infancy and the regret of not being able to give her some proof of my attachment. I could have wished to be of service to you, do not at least let me afflict you. Farewell my poor Fleury, farewell." ~
Vermont Gazette, Bennington, Vermont

MUSINGS

There can never, ever be enough women's shoes!

We have it from unqueſtionable authority, that in the two towns, Lynn and Reading, in Maſſachuſetts, there are conſtantly fifteen hundred perſons employed in manufacturing women's ſhoes. From the product of their labour are annually exported from thence, to different parts of this continent, 450,000 pair of ſhoes, which makes a ſaving to the United States from the foreign importations of this article at 4/6 a pair, of 337,500 dollars ; and they can afford their ſhoes on lower terms than can be imported.

National Gazette, Philadelphia PA, **March 30, 1793**

1794

197. 1794, Dolley Madison marries her second husband, James Madison in 1794. Dolley will be the First Lady of the United States from 1809-1817

198. News from France on the status of women's rights in the newspaper. I've transcribed the article in case it is difficult to read: *January 30, 1794 – "The discussion on some of the articles of the civil code, which had been adjourned was resumed. One of them, which gave women a right to manage, in common with their husbands, their common property, was supported by Lecointre Puyraveaux and decreed to the great satisfaction of the female citizens in the galleries."*

Sunday, Oct. 27.

The difcuffion on fome of the articles of the civil code, which had been adjourned, was refumed. One of them, which gave women a right to manage, in common with their hufbands, their common property, was fupported by Lecointre Puyraveaux, and decreed, to the great fatisfaction of the female citizens in the galleries.

199. I found this quite amusing. As if a beard makes a person more intelligent! _ February 22, 1794 – *"(Paris) The section of the Armed Men in Paris, having desired to know what will be the Republican mode of burying the citizens; the Council of the Commons resolved, that a civil commissioner, wearing a red cap, shall precede all burials.*

A deputation of women with red caps appeared yesterday at the bar of the commune. This new sight in the middle of the council of the commons excited violent murmurs in the tribunes. The president called them to order.

And I cried Chaumette move for the civic mention of the conduct of the tribunes, who show their contempt for abominable women, who desire to appear as men. Is it the part of women to make motions? Does it belong to women to put themselves at the heads of battalions? If there lived in former times a Joan d' Arc (Maid of Orleans), there then lived likewise a Charles VII.

Women are by nature destined to take care of family concerns; to be mothers, to support and rear their children. Our wives should be at home when we are here. If nature willed that women should be men, nature would have given women beards. I move that the deputation of women be not heard. (Motion adopted).

The women immediately put their red caps into their pockets, and withdrew, without giving the least hint of the cause of their visit to the commons.

Chaumette has complained to the municipality that the women of the town are now becoming devotees; that they continue to honor Jesus Christ in the churches and that the enemies of liberty bribe these women to share in their treasonable plots."

"It was generally imagined that Madame du Barry was arrested for the purpose of making her give an account of her fortune, but some papers are said to be found in her possession relative to a plot to destroy the republic together with letters from a number of immigrants whom she

supports. These papers have been sent to the revolutionary tribunal, and she will shortly be tried." ~ **The Philadelphia Inquirer, Pennsylvania**

200. Women were punished for the craziest things in history all around the world. This took place in 1794 Ireland:

February 27, 1794 – "The re-capture of Toulon, France was celebrated here in a singular manner. Milhaud, the National Deputy, ordered three hundred women who had been convicted of correspondence with emigrants, and condemned to die, to be brought from the prison to the square, where the instrument of death is erected. The scene was in the highest degree affecting. The women drowned in tears advanced to the fatal scaffold, on which the executioners stood prepared to administer the fatal blow. The people in great numbers beheld the terrific scene with awful silence.

Milhaud mounting the scaffold, addressed the women in a speech in which he pointed out to them the error of their conduct and the danger in which their measures tended to involve the republic.

He concluded his address by ordering the executioners to knock-off the fetters of the women, all of whom he set at liberty and pardoned." ~ **The Northern Star, Belfast, N. Ireland**

201. On May 7, 1794 Jane Mecom, sister of Benjamin Franklin dies.

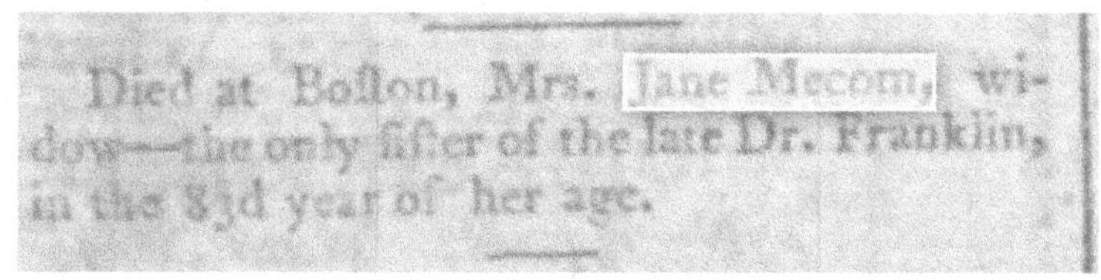

The Philadelphia Inquirer, May 16, 1794

According to her biographer Jane boiled soap and took in boarders to earn money. She and her husband had twelve children but only one of her children outlived her. She and two of her daughters, Jenny and Polly started a small shop selling caps and bonnets. Much of what we know about her is from actual letters sent between her and her brother Benjamin for sixty years, until Benjamin Franklins death in 1790.

202. In **July of 1794** the Governor of the Commonwealth of Virginia, Henry Lee, made a rare and public appeal for the safe return of Peggy Howell's children (a black woman).

July 16, 1794 – *"United States, (Richmond, VA) By the Governor of the commonwealth of Virginia, a Proclamation whereas I have received information that some wicked and evil disposed person or persons, whose names are unknown, did, during the night, feloniously steal and take away two children of Peggy Howell. A free mulatto living in the county of Charlotte with a design as it is supposed, to sell them in some of the neighboring states as slaves. And whereas the rights of humanity are deeply interested in the restoration of the children to their parent, and the order of society is involved in the punishment of the offenders I do by the advice of the Council of State, issue this my Proclamation, offering a reward of fifty dollars for the recovery of each of the said children and the further sum of one hundred dollars for apprehending and securing in the public jail of Charlotte County the offenders.*

Given under my hand as Governor, Henry Lee

(N.B.) The children were both boys between four and five years old. One named Peter, the other named Edmond." ~ **Gazette of the United States, Philadelphia,**

203. *The Battle of Fleurus took place in 1794 Belgium and was considered a significant battle during the French Revolutionary War. News would sometimes take months to get to the states.

1795

February 25, 1795 – The Battle of Fleurus was a major battle fought during the French Revolutionary Wars. *"The Battle of Fleurus. We have already observed, that during the first attack made by the enemies, the female citizens had set an example of devoted zeal. They took up the wounded and carried them on mattresses and in their arms. They dressed their wounds and many of themselves were wounded.*

The female citizen Grumiau, daughter of a municipal officer, being stronger than her companions, carried them alone to the hospital and this girls brother had been killed at her side." ~ **Aurora General Advertiser, Philadelphia, PA, Feb 25, 1795**

204. Women in the Americas had to take their case to court to get any form of payment or pension for their military service: *April 4, 1795 – "A female citizen appeared at the court upon crutches. Having devoted herself to the care of the sick in the advanced post of the army she had her thigh broke by a bomb shell. She prays for relief. Referred to a committee directed to report back tomorrow."* ~ Aurora General Advertiser, Philadelphia, PA

205. This is from the year 1795. Sound familiar? *"Why women and always women in every popular movement? Why daring petitioners, directed by golden wires by no means imperceptible to the thinking man, to the patriot, come to insult the national representation, alluding to those who petitioned for more bread, which is ever occupied in providing for their wants; why do turbulent women excite them in their clamors, by their applause, by their cries, by their vociferations? [...] When will there be an end to this female aristocracy? Our laws grant no political rights to women; well! Why are they everywhere? Why are they in every political assembly? Would it not be reasonable and decent to exclude them? Will public concerns remain a secret if none but male citizens are admitted? Do not the duties of women call them to the bosoms of their families to the practice of domestic virtues, to the education of their children?"* ~ The Philadelphia Inquirer, Pennsylvania, May 23, 1795

206. Judith Sargent Murray, author of 'The Medium', written in 1795, is thought to be the **first** American author to be produced on the stage with her play called "The Medium".

207. A list of books published in June of 1795: – Just Published. *"Ladies Library: Second American edition of Miss Moor's Essays; Lady Pennington's Unfortunate Mother, Mrs. Chapone's Letter on the Government of the Temper, Swift's Letter to a Young Lady Newly Married and Moore's Fables for the Female Sex."* ~ Philadelphia Inquirer, PA

1796

Tennessee becomes the 16th state when it joins the
"Union" on June 1, 1796.

1797

John Adams becomes President of the United States on **March 4, 1797**.
Thomas Jefferson is now the Vice President of the United States.

208. Abigail Adams becomes First Lady. She is 52 years old.

Vice President Thomas Jefferson is a widower.

*"Several women (at least thirteen) who were not presidents'
wives have served as first lady, as when the president was a
bachelor or widower, or when the wife of the president was
unable to fulfill the duties of the first lady herself. In these cases,
the position has been filled by a female relative or friend of the
president, such as:*

Jefferson's daughter Martha Jefferson Randolph

*Jackson's daughter-in-law Sarah Yorke Jackson and his wife's
niece Emily Donelson*

Taylor's daughter Mary Elizabeth Bliss

Benjamin Harrison's daughter Mary Harrison McKee

Buchanan's niece Harriet Lane

Cleveland's sister Rose Cleveland"

209.   First Lady Abigail Adams missed her husband's presidential inauguration as she was reportedly tending to his dying mother.

210.   1797 - The Mona Lisa painting has taken up residence at the Louvre in Paris.

211.   March 31, 1797 – Elizabeth Betty Washington Lewis, sister to President George Washington dies at age 63. She was born in 1733 in Virginia. She is buried at the Western View Plantation in Culpeper, Virginia

212.   April 13, 1797 – [I am including here the books authored by the women only.]

"Lately Books of Publish."

Fille de Chambre, by Mrs. Rowson of the new theater.
Mysteries of Udolpho, by Mrs. Ratcliffe
Poems, by Phillis Wheatley, an African."

Poems, by Phillis Wheatley, an African.

~ The Weekly Franklin Repository, Chambersburg, Pennsylvania

213. In **September of 1797** the celebrated author Mary Wollstonecraft Godwin author of 'The Rights of Women' dies from complications of childbirth to her daughter Mary Shelley, author of Frankenstein. She was just 38 years old. Mary Shelley was born on August 30, 1797.

DIED, lately in England, in child-bed, Mrs. Godwin ; more known as Mifs Wolftonecraft, the celebrated au-thorefs of The rights of Women.

Mary Wollstonecraft was born in 1759 London. At age nine she was enrolled in the local school where she learned to read and write.

In 1784, Mary, along with her sister, opened a school. Mary would publish her first book, 'Thoughts On the Education of Girls' in 1787, followed by her first fictional novel, 'Mary: A Fiction' in 1788. A year later in 1789 she published a political pamphlet entitled 'A Vindication of the Rights of Man'. It was in this pamphlet that Mary aired her grievances against slavery, spoke about the need for a revolution and all of the wrongs in society at the time.

Her most infamous book was published in 1792 at the age of 33. She called it, 'A Vindication of the Rights of Women'. The books main premise was calling for equality among the sexes.

Seeking a revolution, Mary set off for Paris in 1792. By February of 1793 France had declared war on Britain and when Mary tried to leave the country she was denied. During her time in France she wrote 'An Historical and Moral View of the Origin and Progress of the French Revolution; published that year.

Returning to England in 1795 she met and married William Godwin in March of 1797. She gave birth to her daughter, Mary W. Godwin Shelley (author of Frankenstein) in August 1797. An infection, acquired during childbirth, took the life of Mary in September. She was just 38 years old.

In later years Mary Wollstonecraft Godwin would become known as THE FIRST FEMINIST. She is buried at the family tomb at St. Peters, Bournmouth.

214. October 19, 1797

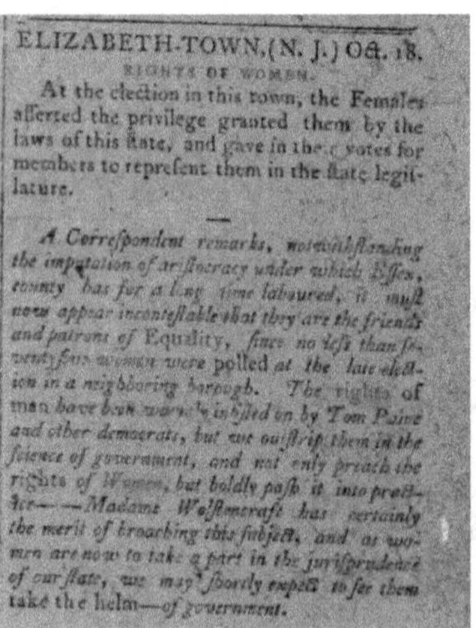

The women were allowed to vote in a local election in Elizabeth Town, New Jersey.

October 19, 1797 – "*(Elizabeth-Town, New Jersey) At the election in this town, the females asserted the privilege granted them by the laws of this state, and gave in the state legislature.*

A correspondent remarks notwithstanding the imputation of aristocracy under which Essex County has for a long time labored, it must now appear incontestable that they are the friends and patrons of Equality since no less than seventy-five women were polled at the late election in a neighboring borough.

The rights of man have been insisted on by Tom Paine and other democrats but we outstrip them in the science of government and not only preach the rights of women, but boldly push it into practice. Madame Wolstencraft has certainly the merit of broaching this subject, and as women are now to take part in the jurisprudence of our state. We may shortly see them take the helm of government." ~ **Gazette of the United States Washington DC**

215. Isabella "Belle" Baumfree is born sometime in the year of 1797 in Swartekill, New York. There are conflicting reports about her date of birth (age). I am using the birth year on her headstone as well as many places, such as the National Women's History Museum, documenting it as the year 1797. Many articles I found placed her year of birth as early as 1775 and stating her age when she passed away as 108 but I am not sure that is correct.

As an adult she changed her name to Sojourner Truth. Sojourner was born a slave but lived in New York, which, unlike the southern states, ended slavery in 1827 when she was approximately thirty years old. We will hear more from Sojourner Truth in the 1800s for her many speaking engagements.

MUSINGS

A milk-woman, who had ferved that article for many years in the neighbourhood of Berwick-ftreet, Soho, died a few days ago, leaving her trade and her clothes to her fervant, a young Irifh-woman, who had been for fome time courted by a lad of her own country ; and, that joy and forrow fhould go hand in hand, from the principle of œconomy, they agreed to marry the fame day that the old woman died, and made the funeral bake-meats ferve for the wedding fupper.

The Evening Mail, London, England, Jan 23, 1797

1798

216. June 1798 - *"Miss Keating, daughter of Colonel Keating, member for Kildare, a fine young woman about 22 years of age, and esteemed* **the First Horse Woman in Ireland**, *is the person who heads the rebels in the county of Kildare. She retired a few days since to the Bog of Allen and has not yet been taken. The troops have burnt her brothers house in revenge."* ~ Ipswich Journal, Ipswich, England

217. *November 16, 1798 – "(**Curious Historical Fact**) "During the troubles in the reign of Charles the Ist (1600-1649) a country girl came to London in search of a place as a servant maid, but not succeeding, she applied herself to carrying out beer from a brew house, and was one of those then called tub women. The brewer observing a well looking girl in this low occupation took her into the family as a servant maid, and after a while married her, be he died while she was yet a young woman, and left her a large fortune.*

The business of the brewer was dropped and the young woman was recommended to Mr. Hyde, a gentleman of skill in the law to settle her husband's affairs. Hyde, who was afterwards the great Earl of Clarendon. Finding the widow's fortune very considerable he married her. Of this marriage there was no other issue than a daughter, who was afterwards the wife of James II and mother of Mary and Ann; Queens of England."

218. *"Madame Buonaparte. The connection between Buonaparte and Barras, the French Director, arose from the following circumstance. Barras conceived a strong partiality for the fortune and person of a Mulatto widow, who married a second time to a French Nobleman. Barras soon contrived to send the Nobleman into the other world and obtained possession of his widow. In time Barras grew tired of her and offered to procure Buonaparte military promotion if he would marry her. Buonaparte had no delicate repugnance, but readily closed with the proposal and, by the interest of Barras was feat with a command to Italy. In consequence of this humane and delicate arrangement, the Mulatto widow is now Madame Buonaparte, and her husband is the Arbiter of Italy."* ~ **Green Mountain Patriot, Peacham, Vermont, Nov 16, 1798**

MUSINGS

Philadelphia Inquirer, Nov 13, 1798 *"Amongst other curiosities exhibited by a travelling showman in a country village, is a mummy hand of Cleopatra, Queen of Egypt, and the arm of Lot's wife."*

1799

FYI - <u>January 26, 1799</u> Advertisement:

A number of healthy German
MEN and WOMEN Redemptioners, (among
which are several Mechanics) just arrived in
LANCASTER, and to be sold for a term of
years   Apply to
            ADAM REIGART, Jun.
Sept. 29, 1798.

"A number of healthy German men and women redemptioners, among which are several mechanics, just arrived in Lanaster, and to be sold for a term of years. Apply to Adam Reigart." ~ Lancaster Intelligencery, Lancaster, PA

219. 1799 - : married women were being treated as underage children by what was called the Doctrine of Coverture which dictated that when a woman married she became under the control of her husband and gave up all legal rights of herself and her property. It stated:

"By marriage, the husband and wife are one person in law: that is, the very being or legal existence of the woman is suspended during the marriage. The husband of a married woman became the owner of any property she brought into a marriage. Further, she could not sign contracts, operate a business in her own name, or retain custody of their children in the event of a divorce."

220. Rest In Peace Priscilla

A free negro woman, a maiden, named Priscilla Wragg, lately died at St. Jago de la Vega, (Jamaica,) in the 121st year of her age. Till the hour of her death she enjoyed the perfect possession of her sight, hearing, and appetite. Her memory was retentive, and such was her loquacity that she literally died talking.

The Observer, London, England, Mar 24, 1799

221. September 29, 1799 – "Mrs. Simpson is now the Postmistress of Chelmsford." ~ **The Observer, London, England**

222. *November 4, 1799 – "**THE FEMALE WARRIORS,** An essay by Dr. Goldsmith: "[...] The proportion which the number of females born in these kingdoms bears to the male children, is, I think, supposed to be as thirteen to fourteen. But as women are not so subject as the other sex to accidents and intemperance, in numbering adults we shall fin the balance on the female side. If in calculating the numbers of the people we take in the multitudes that immigrate to the plantations from whence they never returned. Those that die at sea and the slate of men lost to war. If this be the case, there must be a surplus of the other sex amounting to the same number and this surplus will consist of women able to bear arms, **as I take it for granted, that all those who are fit to bear children are likewise fit to bear arms.***

Now as we have seen the nation governed by old women, I hope to make it appear that it may be descended by young women and surely this scheme will not be rejected as unnecessary as such a juncture when our armies in the four quarter of the globe are in want of recruits; when we find ourselves entangled in a new war with Spain, on the eve of a rupture in Italy and indeed in a fair way of being obliged to make head against all the great potentates of Europe.

But before I unfold my design, it may be necessary to obviate from experience as well as argument the objections which may be made to the delicate frame and tender disposition of the female sex rendering them incapable of the toils and insuperably averse to the horrors of war.

[...] We are informed by Homer, that Penthefilea, Queen of the Amazons, acted as auxiliary to Priam, and fell valiantly fighting in his cause before the walls of Troy. [...] there was a nation of female warriors in Africa, who fought against the Lybian Hercules.

We read in the voyages of Columbus that one of the Carribee Islands was possessed by a tribe of female warriors who kept all the neighboring Indians in awe, but we need not go further than our own age and country to prove that the spirit and constitution of the fair sex are equal to the dangers and fatigues of war.

Every novice who has read the authentic and important history of the pirates is well acquainted with the exploits of two heroines called

Mary Read and Anne Bonny. I myself have had the honor to drink with Anne Cassier, alias Mother Wade who had distinguished herself among the buccaneers of America and in her old age kept a punch house in Port Royal of Jamaica. I have likewise conversed with Moll Davis, who had served as a dragoon in all Queen Anne's wars and was admitted on the pension of Chelsea. The late war with Spain, and even the present, hath produced instances of females enlisting both in the land and sea service and behaving with remarkable bravery in the disguise of the other sex. And who has not heard of the celebrated Jenny Cameron, and some other enterprising ladies of North Britain who attended a certain adventurer in all his expeditions and headed their respective clans in a military character?

That strength of body is often equal to the courage of mind implanted in the fair sex will not be denied by those who have seen the water women of Plymouth, the female drudges of Ireland, Wales and Scotland, the fishwomen of Billingsgate, the weeders, podders, and hoppers who swarm in the fields, and the bunters who swagger in the streets of London; not to mention the indefatigable trulls who follow the camp and keep up with the line of march, though loaded with bantlings and other baggage.

There is scarcely a street in this metropolis without one or more viragos who discipline their husband and domineer over the whole neighborhood. Many months are not elapsed since I was witness to a pitched battle between two athletic females who fought with equal skill and fury until one of them gave out after having sustained seven falls on the hard stones. They were both stripped to the under petticoat. Their breasts were carefully swathed with handkerchiefs and as no vestiges of features were to be seen in either when I came up, I imagined the combatants were of the other sex until a bystander assured me of the contrary giving me to understand that the conqueror has lain in about five weeks of twin bastards, begot by her second, who was an Irish chairman. When I see the avenues of the Strand beset every night with troops of fierce Amazons, who, with dreadful imprecations, stop and beat and plunder passengers, I cannot help wishing that such martial talents were converted to the benefit of the public and those who are so loaded with temporal fire, and so little afraid of eternal fire, should, instead of ruining the souls and bodies of their fellow citizens, be put in a way of turning their destructive qualities against the enemies of the nation.

Having thus demonstrated that the fair sex are not deficient in strength and resolution, I would humbly propose that as there is an excess on their side in quantity to the amount of one hundred thousand part of that number may be employed in recruiting the army as well as in raising thirty new Amazonian regiments, to be commanded by females and serve in regimentals adapted to their sex. The Amazons of old, appeared with the left breast bare, an open jacket, and trowsers that descended no farther than the knee. The right breast was destroyed, that it might not impede them in bending the bow or darting the javelin but there is no occasion for this cruel excision in the present discipline as we have seen instances of women who handle the musquet without finding any inconvenience from that protuberance.

As the sex love gaiety, they may be clothes in vests of pink satin and open drawers of the same with buckskins on their feet and legs. Their hair tied behind and floating on their shoulders and their hats adorned with white feathers. They may be armed with long bayonets, without the encumbrance of swords or shoulder belts. I make no doubt but many young ladies of figure and fashion will undertake to raise companies at their own expense; provided they like their colonels. But I must insist upon it, if this scheme should be embraced, that Mr. Henriquez's seven blessed daughters may be provided with commissions as the project is in some measure owing to the hints of that venerable patriot. I more over give it as my opinion, that Mrs. Kitty Fisher shall have the command of a battalion, and the nomination of her own officers, provided she will warrant them all found and be content to wear proper badges of distinction.

A female brigade, properly disciplined would not, I am persuaded, be afraid to charge a numerous body of the enemy over whom they would have a manifest advantage, for if the barbarous Scythians were shamed to fight with the Amazons who invaded them, surely the French, who pique themselves on their sensibility and devotion to the fair sex would not act upon the offensive a against a band of female warriors arrayed in all the charms of youth and beauty." ~ **Farmers Literary Gazette, Walpole, New Hampshire**

223. A brave woman named Martha:

RUNAWAY. "A Negro woman named Martha, about 48 years of age, a little grey about the forehead and temples, but remarkably healthy and active, of a common size, and is apt to be saucy and use bad language, a remarkable fine cook and spinner and can likewise plow and cart well, a good reaper and binder. She has lived several years in the neighborhood of Duck Creek and has passed for a free woman which I intended to secure to her had she not treated me with such shameful ingratitude, she has been heard cursing and abusing me. I have sufficient evidence of her having persuaded another fellow to leave me, who is a son of hers and I have sufficient reasons to believe she intended to take all the rest of her children from me in like manner as fast as they grew up to age. This being the case I should suppose the most religious people would not think themselves justified in assisting her in escaping or securing her escape as justice is due all sides. They went off together about the middle of September last, I suppose either for Philadelphia or Jersey. Whoever takes up and secures said Negroes so that this subscriber may get them again, shall have $100 reward. Sixty dollars for the fellow and forty for the wench. Signed Henry Trulock." **Aurora General Advertiser, Philadelphia, PA**

How fitting we would end the 1700s with Martha. A brave and courageous woman risking everything to find her freedom. I don't know what happened to Martha, or most of the other runaway slaves but her story is important to acknowledge as she had so much more to gain and so much more to lose.

The 1800s

We will move into the 1800s in Volume II of our journey into women's history. Some of the women introduced to you in the 1700s will make the news again during the 1800s. As we move closer to modern times there are, of course, more and more women's firsts to write about and celebrate!

ABOUT THE AUTHOR

Author: Paula C. Henderson
Visit the author's Women in History Series on Amazon:
https://amzn.to/37F6l0n